HORSEKEEPERS

D0726292

W. H. Walter's

HORSEKEEPERS ENCYCLOPEDIA

Revised and edited by
Chris May, B.Vet.Med., M.R.C.V.S.

Illustrated by
Christine Bousfield and with breed
drawings by Shona Grant

PAPERFRONTS
ELLIOT RIGHT WAY BOOKS
KINGSWOOD, SURREY, U.K.

Typeset in 10/10½pt Times
by County Typesetters, Margate, Kent

Made and Printed in Great Britain by
Richard Clay Ltd., Bungay, Suffolk.

CONTENTS

1

BREEDS AND TYPES OF HORSES AND PONIES

The following are the principal breeds and types, under their recognised classifications.

HEAVY DRAUGHT HORSES

Shire. (Illustrated on page 42.) This is the largest breed in the country, the stallion averaging 17 hands in height, the mare slightly less, and weighing up to one ton. Not unexpectedly in animals of this size, both sexes are normally of docile temperament. Practically all whole colours are met, but chestnut and cream are not favoured, and the original black is becoming rarer. A feature of the breed is the profuse flat, silky hair, or "feathering" at the sides and back of the strong, massive legs.

The Shire traces its history back to the Old English War Horse, which claimed descent from the Chariot Horse of Ancient Britain; this original ancestor, a much smaller animal, was crossed with foreign stock to produce a massive steed capable of carrying the immense weight of an armoured rider, together with its own protective plating. Such was the noble descent of the dray-horse of later times.

Clydesdale. (Illustrated on page 98.) The Clydesdale might be called the Shire Horse of Scotland. It is, however, a lighter and more active type, ranging from 16 to 17 hands, and giving an impression of strength without unnecessary weight. The feathering, confined to the back of the legs, is finer and less plentiful than the Shire's. Whilst some chestnuts and blacks are found, the usual colours are bay and brown, with a white face or a blaze, and white legs from the knees and hocks downward, although the forelegs are sometimes dark-coloured. The face has a flat profile and the head is set on a long, well-arched neck.

This breed is noted for the wearing qualities of its feet and legs, possibly due in some measure to its fairly long, sloping pasterns, which reduce the effects of concussion. Another important characteristic of the Clydesdale is its free, elastic action, which made it particularly suited for farm work, where a good, even and energetic walker was a great asset.

The breed has probably been built up mainly on a variety of Continental types, in conjunction with native Scottish breeds.

Suffolk. (Illustrated on page 105.) Lighter and more active than either the Shire or the Clydesdale, averaging only 16 hands, this horse was chiefly used in agriculture, being invaluable for. slow work on heavy land, but is suited for a variety of purposes, having even produced excellent hunters when crossed with Thoroughbred stallions. The "Suffolk Punch", as it is commonly called on account of its build, can be instantly recognised by its massive neck, "square" body, and the absence of feathering except for a tuft of hair on the fetlock. It always breeds true to colour – chestnut – although this may vary in shade. A hardy constitution enables it to thrive where another breed would fail.

The origin of the Suffolk is uncertain, but there is no doubt it has been bred in East Anglia for about 500 years.

British Percheron. (Illustrated on page 35.) The Percheron originated in France and was not bred in England until after the 1914–18 war. Although easily distinguishable from the Suffolk Punch, it is similar in conformation, strongly built, wide and deep, but slightly taller; stallions should not measure under 16 hands 3 inches, mares not under 16 hands 1 inch. The head is large but well-proportioned, with full, docile eyes and an intelligent expression. Black and grey are the usual colours, no stallion of any other colour being accepted for the Stud Book. The Percheron has a reputation for activity and a capacity for long hours of hard work.

LIGHT DRAUGHT HORSES

Cleveland Bay. (Illustrated on page 196.) A large type of carriage horse, standing between 15 hands 3 inches and 16 hands 2 inches, the Cleveland was for long regarded as a "general utility" horse, working in stage coach teams, on farms, as vanners and under saddle. On account of its handsome appearance and reliability it is always sought for use in State carriages. As the name suggests, the colour must be a shade of bay, with black points and, of course, black mane and tail; there may be a dark stripe ("list") along the back. White on the legs or feet, or as a blaze on the face, may be regarded as indicating the presence of blood of another breed.

Like the Shire, the Cleveland sprang from the Great or War Horse of the fifteenth century, but since those days Thoroughbred and Arab blood have played their parts in its development. Now it is much favoured in the breeding of hunters and other saddle horses, usually being crossed with the Thoroughbred for this purpose. It was formerly used for work on light soils.

Hackney Horse. (Illustrated on page 135.) With its characteristic high action, well arched neck and great trotting speed, the Hackney is the most brilliant and showy of all our harness horses. To meet show ring standards, the natural gait has been developed to give shoulder and hock as well as knee action, the forelegs being well extended and "reaching out" before the feet are put down, the hindlegs well flexed and supplying the necessary propelling power. The Hackney Horse stands on powerful, short legs, and his height usually varies from 15 to 15 hands 2 inches, although 16 hands is not uncommon. There are all colours, but greys are rare.

Although the breed has existed for over two centuries, it is only of comparatively recent years that it has been recognised in its present form, the first Hackney Stud Book being issued many years ago. Its ancestors were probably the old "trotting mares" mated with Arabs. By reason of an ability to "go for ever" at its natural pace, the trot, it was a useful riding horse, but in present days its main purpose is show ring work.

Hackney Pony. Being closely associated with the Hackney

Horse, this pony must be considered under the heading of Light Draught Horses. The same show action is expected of the Pony as of its larger relative. In height it should not exceed 14 hands 2 inches, and chestnut, bay and brown are the colours most frequently seen.

Native ponies were used in its development, Welsh mares playing the largest part. As is to be expected from such blood, great endurance and courage, combined with docility, are features of the breed. The Hackney Pony should not be confused with the cob-type of Welsh Pony, which is quite distinct from it.

SADDLE HORSES

Arab. (Illustrated on page 89.) This beautiful breed could be summed up briefly by the words: "Quality, gracefulness and courage combined with docility and intelligence". In appearance it is distinguished by the small, neat head with dished profile, small ears, large nostrils and eyes, the arched neck and fine mane, and gracefully carried silky tail. The height rarely exceeds 15 hands, and the usual colours are chestnut, bay, white or grey, frequently brown, but seldom black. Anglo-and Part-Bred Arabs, as well as Pure-Breds, are registered by the Arab Horse Society.

This horse came to us from the deserts of Arabia and became the foundation of the English Thoroughbred.

Thoroughbred. (Illustrated on page 121.) The term "Thoroughbred" should not be confused with "Pure-bred". Strictly, it applies only to horses with both parents registered in the General Stud Book, and is synonymous with the term "Racehorse".

In former days, horses began their racing lives much later than today. Nowadays, for financial reasons, they are required to run as two-year-olds. This has led to a system of management whereby they are "forced" into early maturity, producing taller and faster *sprinters*, in many cases at the expense of stamina.

The usual height is about 16 hands, although some are under this and others exceed 17 hands. Colours vary, but chestnut, bay and brown seem to be most common, although there have been many good greys. The head should be lean and fine, with prominent, intelligent eyes, and the whole appearance suggests speed and alertness.

The modern Thoroughbred traces its decent back to three Eastern Stallions brought to England in the late seventeenth and early eighteenth centuries – the Byerley Turk, The Darley Arabian and the Godolphin Barb – but it must not be forgotten that other Eastern Blood had been introduced before that time.

Hunter. (Illustrated on page 80.) Being a type, not a distinct breed, it is difficult to lay down standards for size and colour. In selecting a hunter, choice must be governed largely by the type of country; open well-drained grassland calling for a lighter framed Thoroughbred type of hunter, while heavier soils with a high proportion of arable farming are more suited to a heavier and sturdier type of horse. The Thoroughbred takes a great share in hunter-breeding, many hunters being

Welsh Mountain Pony

actually of this strain whilst others are the offspring of Thoroughbred sires and draught mares (particularly the Cleveland Bay and Irish Draught). The inclusion of Arab blood is very desirable, transmitting, as it does, the stamina required to stand up to hardship; the tendency towards lightness in the leg rectifies itself after the first cross. What is needed is a horse that moves freely at all paces, can gallop on, jump confidently and stand up to work. Colour is, of course, a matter of individual preference, but light chestnuts and roans are least in demand. In the past, some of the finest hunters were imported from Ireland where the soil and climate are ideal for their breeding. Today, nearly all hunters are home-bred – Thoroughbred stallions being used to produce the lighter types, while Irish Draught stallions or those of other larger breeds (such as the Hanovarian) are used to produce the bigger and more sturdy types of hunter.

Hack. The term can be loosely employed to describe almost any sort of horse, of whatever shape, size or colour, ridden for pleasure, that is, hacking. It is frequently but ignorantly used in a derogatory sense. When considering the Show Hack, however, one must look for a certain, high standard. A small Thoroughbred, or an animal showing a good proportion of that blood, is favoured, not exceeding 15 hands 2 inches, and with good, free action. Given all the necessary qualifications as to conformation, quality and action, it will fail in the Show Ring unless properly schooled; perfect manners are essential.

Polo Pony. This is a pony in name only. At one time the height limit was 14 hands 2 inches, but now there is no restriction. It is usually of the well-bred Hunter type, and many good ponies have Welsh Cob blood. Some of our best Polo Ponies were bred in the Argentine from stock crossed with English blood.

Cobs. (Illustrated on page 51.) With the exception of the Welsh Cob, which is a distinct breed of pony, the term "Cob" refers to any animal between the heights of 14 and 15 hands, that is, between pony and horse size. It is also necessary that the animal be sturdy and strongly-built (hence the adjective "cobby" applied to a horse of similar build). The "weight-carrying cob", it is worth noting, makes an excellent Hack or Hunter.

PONIES

Connemara. The Connemara is a very hardy, compact, short-legged pony from the West of Ireland, standing between 13 and 14 hands. Grey is the most popular colour, with black, brown and bay slightly less common, whilst the original typical dun is not so often seen now; chestnut and roan are rare.

The history of the breed dates back several centuries to a hardy type of pony which existed in Western Ireland, the Connemara of today indicating the addition of Arab blood. The Connemara Pony Breeders' Society, formed in 1923, has successfully worked for the improvement of the breed by careful selective breeding, and today shows an encouraging increase in the number of registered stallions and mares.

Dales. (Illustrated on page 26.) The best description of the Dales Pony would be "a miniature cart horse"; in fact, it probably descended from an original native breed of cart horse, and Clydesdale blood has been used for added strength and weight. The height does not exceed 14 hands 2 inches, and the favoured colours are black, bay, brown and grey, others pointing to crossing. Possessing great powers of endurance, it is generally docile and easily broken-in, and is equally suitable for riding or driving. The well-arched neck is short and thick, the back strong and straight, the legs and feet ideal, with a quality of fine hair at the heels. Its outstanding characteristics include sureness of foot and marked trotting abilities.

Dartmoor. (Illustrated on page 160.) The Dartmoor is popular as a child's pony when properly handled in the early stages and not corn fed (as with most ponies, oats make it difficult to manage). Its height should not exceed 12 hands 2 inches, and its favoured colours are bay, brown or black. The head should be small and clean-cut, with an appearance of intelligence.

Haphazard breeding, due to casual methods of turning out on the moors, has marred the breed considerably in recent years, but the Breed Society and other persons interested are working hard to restore the original type.

Exmoor. (Illustrated on page 67.) As a child's hunter, the smart-looking Exmoor is deservedly popular. Measuring usually under 12 hands 2 inches, it is a little weight-carrier. The head is small, with flat profile, wide forehead and nostrils, small ears, and the light-coloured muzzle, or "mealy nose", as it is appropriately called, which is a distinctive feature of the breed. There should be no feathering about the fetlocks. The colour most commonly found is mousy-brown, but there are some bays and duns. It is a native breed, claiming pure descent, but some authorities are of the opinion that Arab and Thoroughbred blood have been introduced, and its appearance supports that theory. Certainly, however, by judicious crossing, successful hunters and even racehorses have been produced form Exmoor blood.

Fell. (Illustrated on page 20.) There is little difference except in height, between this and the other hardy native pony from the Lake District, the Dales Pony, and in fact they originated as one breed. The Fell is the smaller, seldom exceeding 14 hands, the average being 13 hands 2 inches. The colour may be brown, black, grey, bay or dun, but never chestnut. A short-legged but fast, active animal, it is sturdy and strong, making a good ride and being well able to carry considerable weight. It carries plenty of mane and tail, and the silky hair at the fetlock is typical of the breed.

Highland. (Illustrated on page 170.) The real Highland, or Barra, Pony hails from the Outer Hebrides; two other types (the Mull and the Garron) being offshoots developed by cross-breeding and better conditions. In its natural state the Highland rarely exceeds 12 to 13 hands, but in more favourable circumstances it attains up to 14 hands 2 inches. Though most colours are found, dun and cream are preferred, especially when accompanied by a black "eel stripe" along the back and dark points to the legs. The head is square, being broad between the eyes and short, but with wide nostrils and "dished" face; it has a pleasing neck. Its chief virtues lie in its gentleness, intelligence, sureness of foot and strength. A hardy constitution enables the Highland Pony to live out all the year round on indifferent pasture.

The heavier, Mainland type, is useful for weight-carrying over difficult country and for hill-farm work, whilst the lighter Barra makes an ideal, reliable, child's pony besides being suitable for farm work and driving.

New Forest. (Illustrated on page 74.) The New Forest Pony is not an outstanding beauty; its general appearance, with short neck and fairly large head, is often described as "common". All colours are found, but mostly bay and brown. Sure-footed, easily broken-in and quickly becoming traffic-proof, the New Forest makes an excellent mount for a child and, at the same time, is a willing, useful harness pony. Living out on the Forest, fending for itself, it may not grow above 13 hands, whilst with better feeding and care it may reach 14 hands or a little over, but it should be mentioned, over-feeding, especially with corn, is inadvisable as it will soon "hot-up".

The breed is not now a pure one, other pony blood having being introduced, but records show that the original type was known in Saxon times.

Shetland. (Illustrated on page 111.) Probably the best-known pony in this country, the Shetland is the smallest and one of the oldest in existence. The maximum height for the Stud Book is 42 inches (measurement is in inches for the Sheltie), the average is 40 inches or less, and the smallest on record 26 inches. At one time there was a theory that, if bred and reared under less rigorous conditions, it would become taller, but this has not been borne out in practice. Almost every colour is met, but white is uncommon, and white markings are not liked.

The Shetland is often condemned as being "a little devil", but well broken and *sensibly* treated it will make a good pony for a child; it is surefooted, intelligent and docile, yet has pluck and is exceptionally strong. The head is fine and small, the body compact, and the mane, forelock and tail long and profuse. Almost as much a characteristic of appearance as the small stature is the thick, long coat. Foals, in winter, are especially well protected against the bitterest weather by a dense woolly undercoat kept dry by an outer coat of long hair.

The Shetland is also remarkable for its long life, many attaining the age of 40 years.

The history of the breed dates back to the earliest times, and the purity of the type throughout the centuries is obviously due to the isolated position of its native home. It was at one time in great demand as a pit pony for deep-working coal mines, but now it is mostly used under saddle.

Welsh Mountain Pony. (Illustrated on page 11.) This hardy, spirited little animal is a native breed with a remarkable resemblance to the Arab. Though seldom exceeding 12 hands, it can easily cope with heavy weights, in saddle or harness, and shows great endurance. The usual colours are grey, brown and bay, with skewbalds and piebalds being disliked. With its appearance, character and good movement, the Welsh Mountain Pony makes an excellent ride, but is particularly valuable for crossing out to breed quality ride-and-drive ponies; a Welsh-Arab cross especially producing good results. Difficult as it is to favour one native breed above another, there is little doubt that the Welshman should head the list for general qualities.

Welsh Pony. This breed does not exceed 13 hands 2 inches and inherits many of the characteristics of the Welsh Mountain Pony, the foundation of the breed of which it is a larger and stronger edition. It was originally produced by crossing the small Welsh Cob with the Mountain Pony. It has been extensively used for hunting on the Welsh hills. It is now a very popular breed of children's pony, but is also bred for hunting and showing.

Welsh Cob. (Illustrated on page 59.) Two sections of the Welsh Stud Book have been set aside for Cobs. Section D is for the Welsh Cob itself, while Section C is devoted to what is now known as the Welsh pony of Cob type, which must be under 13 hands 2 inches. The only difference between these two types, is the larger height and proportionate strength of the Cob (Section D), of which the majority are between 14 hands 2 inches and 15 hands 1 inch. The predominant colours are bay, black, brown, chestnut, and roan, but any colour is permitted except piebald and skewbald. These are a very strong ride-and-drive type of horse which are short-legged and fast trotters. They have silky manes and heel tufts. The breed has been evolved from the native Mountain Pony (which it closely resembles) and from the old Welsh cart horse, by many crosses – including the Thoroughbred. The trotting action also seems to point to a trace of blood from the Hackney, or some similar breed of driving horse.

The number of horses used in agriculture has now fallen almost to zero, whilst the Thoroughbred industry, despite financial difficulties, has gone from strength to strength. However, the majority of horses in Great Britain are used solely for riding, and the staggering increase in their numbers recently allows no argument as to their popularity.

The horse has no equal as a pet for pleasure and recreation.

2

BUYING A HORSE
OR PONY

Buying a horse or pony can be a challenging and exciting enterprise. However, before setting out, it is important to be sure that you have the facilities, and finances, and can commit the time to look after an animal properly.

Having decided that you want to buy a horse, it is most important to have a clear idea of the sort of horse you are looking for. The height and type, or breed, required will depend on your size and weight, the kind of equestrian activity you wish to undertake, your capabilities as a rider and the facilities which you have available to look after it.

A child's pony must be large enough so as not to be outgrown too quickly, yet the child must be able to control it. Likewise, if no stabling is available and the pony must live out with only a shelter to protect it, one of the hardier native breeds will be necessary, rather than an Arab or similar less-hardy animal.

The most suitable type of horse will depend almost entirely on the type of activity for which it will be used and will have to fit the requirements of a hunter, eventer, hack, polo pony, or show horse as required. Above all, decide what sort of horse you want before looking at any that are for sale, and stick to that decision. When you go to look for a hack, don't come home with a racehorse.

Where to Buy. The advertising columns of magazines and local papers swarm with offers of horses for sale. When studying advertisements, be guided not so much by what is said, but by what is left out. The jargon used is often not much help either. 'Recently broken and ready to bring on' may describe a weak, inexperienced horse that is difficult to manage, while 'not a novice ride' could conceal a lunatic! A horse always assumes outstanding qualities when it is put up for sale. It becomes such a paragon of virtue that one marvels that the owner can bear to part with it. Though most people selling horses in this way are genuine, it is sensible always to be slightly suspicious and to judge the horse entirely on its merits, rather than by what you are told.

It is often quite helpful to take someone else along with you to look at a horse advertised for sale – preferably an experienced horseman or woman. A second impartial opinion is often helpful and he or she may pick up points that you have missed. Some animals can be ruled out at first glance because, above all, you must have a 'liking for the horse'. This is a personal thing with which no-one else can help you. However, having decided that you like the look of a horse at first sight, there can be a tendency to only see what you want to see. This is where a friend can be helpful to keep you straight.

It may be that a friend, or a friend-of-a-friend, has a horse for sale. In this case, it will probably be easier to find out more about the horse or pony's past history and capabilities. But horses bought from friends have a tendency to go wrong. As a rule, buying from friends is best avoided if friendship is to be valued.

At the recognised horse sales, there is usually a good selection of horses on offer. The difficulty here is that it is impossible to examine them thoroughly or to try them. Also, many horses end up at horse sales that have been impossible to sell privately. Horses with all kinds of problems, both physical and mental, end up at horse sales, and though genuine bargains can be found, the inexperienced buyer should be extremely wary. This is one market that is best left to the professionals.

There remains the much abused horse-dealer. Strangely, this is often one of the best ways of finding a suitable horse. Horse dealers, like other businessmen, have their reputation to think of if they deal in a large way. It is the 'here today, gone tomorrow'-type of which you should be aware, but remember, the dealer is a businessman and is not working for the good of his health. Find a reliable local one, preferably on recommendation, tell him what you want and how much you intend paying. He will do his best to satisfy you, and will

Fell Pony

usually be able to come up with a choice of horses to suit your needs.

When going to look at a horse, try to examine it as thoroughly as possible. By all means feel its legs, if you know what you are looking for. But if you do not, you will be no wiser than when you started, and will probably have displayed your ignorance into the bargain! Above all, observe the horse closely. Try and assess its temperament. Look carefully at its tack. If it is being ridden in anything other than a simple snaffle bridle, ask yourself why. Have a look at the animal's feet and shoes to see if they have been cared for and are wearing evenly.

When the horse is being ridden for you to watch, remember that it is being ridden by its usual rider who is probably making it do what it is used to, and, usually, what it does best. When you try it, make it do something different – not just a repeat of what the previous rider has done.

Above all, ask questions. Some horses' behaviour can be considerably affected by their feeding, so it is important to know how the horse has been fed and what exercise it has been given. It is also vital to question its owner about its behaviour in traffic and when being clipped, shod, or loaded into a horsebox or trailer. This is the time to find out about problems – not after you have bought the animal.

Trial. Some advertisers and dealers offer horses on trial – often for a period of one or two weeks. This can be very helpful. This will enable you to assess how the horse behaves in its new surroundings, and, if you are an experienced horseman or woman, to thoroughly assess it when being ridden. A week's trial is usually sufficient, and gives the horse a chance to settle into its new surroundings and get used to you handling him. It is not fair to judge the horse for the first day or two, but after this you can try him at the sort of work he is required to do and assess him. If you are happy with the animal, it is sensible then to ask your vet to examine him, to ensure there are no unforeseen problems that are likely to arise, before concluding the deal.

Warranties. A warranty is a statement, either verbally or in writing, concerning a horse's suitability for a purpose or concerning its behaviour. Verbal warranties can be refuted in a legal action, and it is preferable that all warranties should be given in writing.

When taking a written warranty, see that it covers everything with which you are concerned. This may include age, freedom from vices, suitability for a purpose (such as a child's pony or a hunter) and the animal's behaviour, e.g. 'quiet to ride, shoe, load, clip' or 'sensible in traffic'. It should be noted that warranty consists of the description following the words warranted. For example, 'such-and-such a horse, bay mare 14.1 hh warranted quiet to ride', means that the animal's height has not been warranted.

Litigation is at all times an undesirable procedure, but especially in the matter of horses, where the ramifications of the law are so intricate. 'Caveat emptor' – let the buyer beware – is the watchword, and every possible precaution should be taken against buying trouble.

Veterinary Examination. Having found a horse that you like, which you think will suit your purpose and is being offered at a price you are prepared to pay, it is then a sensible precaution to have the animal vetted before you conclude the deal. Pre-purchase veterinary examinations are carried out at the request of the purchaser, not the vendor. It is important, when asking a vet to carry out this examination for you, to tell him exactly what you intend to use the horse for, because he will be examining the animal to see whether or not it is suitable for this purpose.

A standard examination is carried out at the seller's premises where the vet will examine the horse both at rest and at exercise. He or she will be looking for any disease or defect that is likely to affect the animal's usefulness, and will record them on a certificate, together with his opinion as to whether or not they are significant. For instance, minor blemishes may not affect an animal's usefulness as a hack, but could make it totally unsuitable for showing. Finally, the vet will give an opinion on the horse's suitability.

Payment. Terms of payment will be arranged with the seller – deposit on concluding the deal, payment on or before despatch, etc. – but normally the purchaser meets carriage charges and the cost of a veterinary certificate. Payment by the instalment system is also widely used through the services of well-known hire purchase finance companies. Should instalment facilities be offered to you by the owner at his personal risk, you could rest assured he had faith in his animal and wanted a good home for it.

3

TEETH AND AGEING

Signs of Age. The outward appearance of the horse itself is a poor guide to its age; many old horses, from good treatment, appear much younger – and, of course, the reverse applies. It is frequently said that deepening of the hollows above the eyes is an indication of advancing years, but this, apart from being very vague, is also unreliable. Up to 8 years, age may be estimated fairly accurately from the teeth (with experience) by the time of their eruption, wear and general appearance. After this, only a rough estimate is possible.

Terms in Ageing. All Thoroughbreds have their "official birthday" on 1st January, others in the U.K. on 1st May.

The term "rising" means approaching. For example, "rising 6" is "nearer 6 than 5"; "off" means passed, thus, "5 off" is "over 5 but not rising 6". A horse is said to be "aged" when he is over 8 years old.

Other terms in ageing are:

Colt: A young entire horse (uncastrated) under 4 years old.

Filly: A young female horse under 4 years old.

Foal: A young horse of either sex, under 1 year old, i.e. colt-foal or filly-foal.

Yearling: A horse of either sex between 1 and 2 years old.

Gelding: A neutered horse (male but castrated).

Horse: The general term for an animal of either sex, but strictly meaning a stallion.

Mare: A female horse that is 4 years old or more.

Number of Teeth. The adult horse has 40 or 42 teeth, the mare 36 or 38. The variations are due **(a)** to the presence or absence of small "wolf" teeth in the molars, and **(b)** to the frequent absence of canine teeth or tushes in the mare.

The formulae are:

Horse:	Incisors	Canines	Molars	Total
Top Jaw	3 each side	1 each side	6 each side	20
Lower Jaw	3 each side	1 each side	6 each side	20

Mare:	Incisors	Canines	Molars	Total
Top Jaw	3 each side	—	6 each side	18
Lower Jaw	3 each side	—	6 each side	18

The Incisors are the nipping teeth in front, the centre two being the Centrals, the next the Laterals, the last the Corners. There is a space between the Corner Incisors and the Canine teeth, and a further space between the Canines and the cheek teeth (Molars).

INCISORS
(from the side)

1. Centrals
2. Laterals
3. Corners
4. Notch at 7 years
   (the seven-year hook)

SECTION THROUGH TOOTH

1. Infundibulum or "Mark"
2. Enamel
3. Ivory
4. Dental Star or "Fanghole"

Fig. 1   The Teeth

Parts of the Incisor Teeth

Crown: The part of the tooth that is visible above the gum.
Root: The part of the tooth embedded in the jawbone.
Table: The wearing or biting surface of the tooth.
Infundibulum or "Mark": A blackened depression in the centre

of the teeth in young horses. This disappears as the teeth wear down, serving as an indication of age.

Dental Star or "Fanghole": The tip of the pulp cavity (which runs down the middle of the tooth) which becomes exposed by wear in older horses. It appears as an elongated black line in front of the Infundibulum in older horses and becomes progressively more rounded in outline. Its shape and appearance are used to age older horses.

Estimating Age. For purposes of ageing, the lower Incisors are observed; the "Mark" is shallower in these than in the upper Incisors and therefore grows out sooner. Changes in the Tables of the Centrals show a year later in the Laterals, and the following year in the Corners.

TABLE OF ERUPTION AND CHANGES IN THE INCISORS

Temporary Teeth. The milk teeth are small and white with a pronounced neck, and appear as follows:

Birth or soon after:	The two Centrals appear in each jaw.
4 to 8 weeks:	The two Laterals appear in each jaw.
8 to 10 months:	The two Corners appear in each jaw.
12 months:	All temporary teeth are in wear.

Permanent Teeth. The permanent teeth are larger than the temporaries, not so white and without a definite neck.

2¼ to 2½ years:	The Permanent Centrals begin to replace the Temporary Centrals.
Rising 3:	The Central Incisors in both jaws meet at the front edges when the mouth is closed.
3 years:	The Permanent Centrals are in wear.
3½ years:	The Permanent Laterals appear.
4 years:	Laterals and Centrals are level and in wear at the front edges; the "Mark" extends across the Table.
4½ years:	The Corner milk teeth are replaced by Permanents.
4 to 5 years:	The Canines appear.
5 years:	The Corners are in wear on the front edge only; all the adult teeth are now present

Dales Pony

	and the mouth has a neat appearance.
6 years:	All teeth are fully developed and in wear, the "Marks" in the Centrals becoming smaller. The upper Corner Incisor extends beyond the lower Corner Incisor at the back.
Rising 7:	The Tables of the Centrals are becoming triangular – like all Incisors, its outline is altered when lower parts of the teeth are exposed by wear. The "Marks" on the Corners are oblong and show the least wear.
7 years:	The Corner Incisor in the upper jaw shows a notch (sometimes called the 7-year hook) where it projects over the corresponding tooth in the lower jaw. The "Marks" in the Laterals show signs of wearing out.
Rising 8:	In the Centrals, the Dental Star begins to

	show as a line in front of the "Mark". The "Marks" in the Corners are becoming smaller.
8 to 8 off:	All Incisors are becoming triangular.
9 years:	From now on, the teeth become longer and lose their neat, vertical appearance, the angle at which the upper and lower jaws meet becoming less and the teeth projecting forward.

Galvayne's Groove. This is a vertical stain on the outer surface of the Upper Corner Incisors. Not all horses have it, but it is useful in ageing older horses which do. It first appears at the gums at 10 years. By 15 years it has extended half way down the teeth, and by 20 it has reached the whole length of the teeth. Between 20 and 25, the top half of the groove grows out, and it completely disappears again by the time a horse reaches 30.

4

STABLES AND FITTINGS

In many cases, horse-owners will use existing stables, or convert other buildings, rather than construct new stables. Nevertheless, this should not prevent consideration of the form which stabling should take. Remember that before commencing any building or alterations, it is essential to consult your local Council about planning requirements.

Obviously, brick, stone or concrete are the best materials for the construction of stables, although, because they may be damp or cold, they are better lined with wood. This will also help protect the horse from injury. Wooden stables are also perfectly adequate, providing that the walls are thick enough (2.5cm or 1″ minimum) and there is sufficient insulation to keep the horse warm. Concrete or breeze blocks faced with cement are excellent and cheap building materials. Corrugated iron is not suitable for stables; with the possible exception of the construction of a field shelter when no other materials are available.

The best roofing materials are slates or tiles, especially when laid on a felted wooden roof. But matchboarding covered with heavy roofing felt alone is a good substitute, although it may need occasional attention for tears, etc. Corrugated iron, again, makes poor roofing. In addition to its drawbacks already mentioned, there is the objection of dampness from condensation. Asbestos is good from the point of view of reducing fire risks and extremes of temperature, but it cracks easily. Feather-edge boarding is suitable only for temporary shelters since it is never completely weather-proof.

Every effort should be made to provide each horse with a loose-box; that is, a separate "room" where it is at liberty to move freely in the space allowed, instead of being tied up

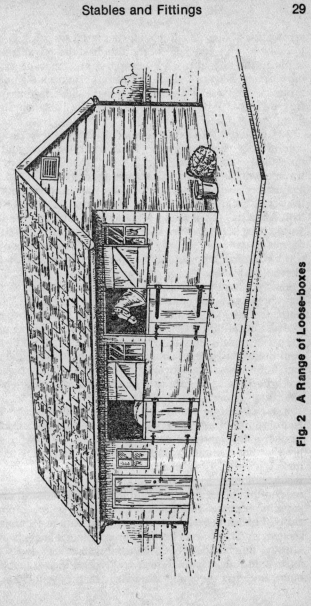

Fig. 2 A Range of Loose-boxes

staring at a blank wall all the time it is inside, as in a stall. The loose-box, with its half-doors, also has the advantage of allowing the animal to look outside. A horse has, or should have, an inquisitive mind, always interested in what is going on around it. Boredom is a great enemy in the stable, leading quite frequently to crib-biting, wind-sucking and other similar stable vices.

A loose-box must be large enough for the horse to turn comfortably without knocking itself, and to lie down and get up with ease and no fear of being "cast", that is, unable to rise when down. Once a horse has had difficulty getting up, the chances are it will be reluctant to lie down again and will not get the necessary amount of rest. A loose-box should not be less than 3.6 metres (12 ft) square for a horse of 15 hands. The door should be at least 2.5 metres (8 ft) high, and wide enough so that there is no danger of the horse knocking itself on the door posts when being led in or out. Stable doors should be at least 1.25 metres (4 ft) wide.

Ideally, all stables should be at least 3 metres (10 ft) high, and they should certainly not be less than 2.5 metres (8 ft). A roof with a span (two roofs meeting at a ridge) is preferable to and provides better ventilation than one with a single sloping roof.

That a stable is cold matters less than that it should be free from draughts. Here, of course, the all-important question of ventilation arises. Gone for ever, it is to be hoped, is the old idea that a horse must be kept in a sort of hot-house atmosphere, particularly at night. The necessity of a constant supply of pure fresh air cannot be too strongly stressed; a stuffy stable is a fruitful source of colds and other ailments. Ammonia, which is produced in large quantities in a stable, is a light gas and quickly fouls the atmosphere, and bad air is irritating to the horse.

Ventilation is particularly important with respect to the build-up of dangerous levels of fungal spores and dust in the stable atmosphere. This can be responsible for a very common cause of ill-health known as Chronic Obstructive Pulmonary Disease, or COPD, which will be described in a later chapter. Affected animals develop a cough because their lungs are sensitive to fungal spores which are released in vast numbers from hay and bedding materials. If the ventilation is inadequate, dangerous levels of spores can build up even when the best hay and straw are used.

It has been estimated that a horse uses up approximately 16,000 cubic feet of air per hour. Merely that amount of space is neither sufficient nor even necessary. It must be remembered that this amount of air is needed hourly and therefore the air must be changed frequently and kept circulating. The air inlets and outlets in a stable should be designed so as to produce a minimum of six complete air changes an hour to ensure satisfactory ventilation. With half-doors and open top partitions this is a simple matter; unless rain or snow are driving in, the top door should always be open, day and night. There will be times, particularly in the British climate, when top doors must be closed, and against such times there will have to be an alternative method of ventilation. An opening window, preferably of the hopper type – that is, hinged to fall inwards – is the answer. With this type of window, the incoming current of air is directed upwards and, being cooler and heavier than the air in the stable, will then descend and in so doing become diffused and warmed, thus avoiding a draught. If louvre ventilation at the ridge of the roof can also be arranged, as an outlet for the lighter, foul air, this is excellent, as free circulation is more easily ensured. Light, being almost as important as ventilation, adds a further reason for windows in the event of the top doors being closed. (See Illustration, page 29.)

A point to remember here is that windows, fastenings, electric light fittings, etc., should be well out of reach of the horse. It is astonishing the irresistible attraction movable objects have for horses; like children, they love to play with things they can "jiggle about" themselves, and the more irritating and monotonous the resulting noise, it seems, the better they like it.

Careful consideration must be given to the flooring and drainage. In deciding the material to be employed, remember that a non-absorbent, hard floor offering good foot-hold is required. The old-fashioned cobble stoned floor was as bad as the flag-paved one; the former did not provide efficient drainage and the latter became dangerously slippery. Asphalt, of course, can be dismissed at once for the same reason. Since such types as grooved Blue Staffordshire bricks, which are ideal for the purpose, are rather costly, we are left with the most common, and possibly the cheapest, concrete. Concrete floors must be of sufficient thickness and strength to avoid cracking and breaking up, laid on about nine inches of rubble, firmly rammed, and with only just enough gentle "fall" or slope to allow drainage (one in forty is sufficient). The finish should not be perfectly smooth, and to improve foot-hold and drainage it is advisable to groove the surface, the "herring bone" pattern being found most suitable. This can be done by drawing a pointed stick along the concrete before it completely dries. The floor, of whatever material, should be higher than the level of the ground or yard outside for the sake of dryness. A drainage channel in the floor is useful and this should lead to a drain outside (not inside) the box.

Fittings. Fittings, such as manger, hay-rack, etc., inside the stable, are best kept to a minimum. Floor space is usually too valuable to be wasted, and the less the number of projections, the less the liability of injury. Wooden mangers are insanitary, being difficult to keep perfectly clean, and the old type of hay rack was usually placed at an inconvenient height which allowed seeds and dust to fall in the horse's eyes, or into its nostrils where they could be inhaled. Automatic water drinkers can save labour but must be checked and maintained regularly. Water buckets on the floor are perfectly satisfactory and their use gives a better idea of the horse's water consumption.

It is quite possible to manage very well with no stable fittings at all, and this has distinct advantages when scrubbing and cleaning the stable. A tie-ring attached to the wall at a height of 1.5 metres (5 ft) is useful to tie the horse up for grooming, or to fix a hay-net. Removable plastic, or better still rubber, mangers can be used for the concentrate ration. Feeding by this means, at floor level, is more natural for the horse (helping any discharges to drain down its nose). Although hay can be fed on the floor, this tends to be very wasteful. A hay-net is preferable and has the added advantage that the hay can be soaked in water to reduce dust and fungal spores.

Food Store. The food store is an important part of the establishment, and one upon which some care and thought should be spent.

It is imperative that this building should be dry, and provide as much protection as possible against vermin. It is not easy to make a forage barn completely vermin-proof and you will soon learn that a cat is no mere mascot in stables. Here a digression from horses may be excused; do remember that even a stable cat needs food and drink, a hungry one does not necessarily make the best ratter.

The position of the barn or food store is worth consideration. Many years ago, it was the custom to build the hay-loft over the boxes or stalls, and a more inconvenient arrangement is difficult to imagine, as you will agree if you have ever been called upon to perform the necessary feats of strength and acrobatics in hauling a ton of hay up to a loft in 40-60 lb bales, later running up and down a usually rickety and highly dangerous ladder every feeding time. This may be grand exercise but occasionally leads to loss of temper and the use of bad language. The best place for storing food is in a ground-floor building close to the stables; a spare loose-box being ideal for small quantities.

A large stock of food is economical and convenient, but only if it can be properly stored. This applies particularly to hay. Concrete floors can never be perfectly dry, and bales should be raised off them on bricks or lengths of timber to allow the air to circulate freely. As a guide to the size of the building, one ton of baled hay, that is, about 50 bales, takes approximately 270 cubic feet of space. Rat-proof corn bins should be provided for other food, such as oats, bran, etc., and even chaff if possible, since vermin cause considerable loss – more from tainting than by what they eat. For concentrates or other feeds in bags, a plastic dustbin (preferably with a lid held on by clips) makes an ideal container for a bag that has been opened.

The food store should be secure, and kept shut and locked at all times to reduce the possibility of horses breaking in and gorging themselves – with potentially serious consequences. (See "Gross Over-eating" on page 213.)

5

STABLE ROUTINE, EXERCISE AND WORK

Daily Routine. With all animals, and possibly most of all with horses, a definite, regular routine is necessary. It is impossible to lay down hard and fast rules; circumstances have to be considered, but commonsense and thought for the animal's well-being and comfort are the foundation of such a routine.

The system must be built around a framework based on the recognition of certain facts. Feeds should be small, regular and frequent, and ample time allowed for their digestion. As a general rule, the daily ration for stabled horses in work should be divided into three feeds. However, animals in hard work will require at least one, and possibly two, more feeds to enable them to cope with a large intake of concentrates. A horse doing light work will often be given a small feed first thing in the morning, with a main feed at midday, after exercise, and a further feed in the early evening. A horse doing little work may receive concentrate feeds in the morning and at night, but may only be given hay at midday.

A typical daily routine for a horse doing light work could be as follows:

7.30–8.00 a.m.	Refill water bucket; refill hay-net; give a small concentrate feed (1–2 kg); muck out and lay back bedding.
9.30 a.m.	Groom; exercise.
12.00 p.m.	Pick up droppings; refill water bucket and hay-net; give main feed.
2.00–4.00 p.m.	Horse left quiet to rest.
4.00 p.m.	Pick up droppings; groom (remove mud and

	sweat which has dried after exercise, and massage); walking exercise in hand, if possible.
5.00 p.m.	Bed down; refill water bucket and hay-net; give third concentrate feed.
10.00 p.m.	Check horse; adjust rugs, etc. (Horses doing hard work can be given a fourth feed at 10.00 p.m.)

Exercise and Work. As a general rule, a fit horse requires two hours' exercise daily, and for a working animal adequate rest is essential. It will have been noticed, in the suggested programme, that a period of two hours is set aside for this purpose.

British Percheron

The greater part of the exercise should be carried out at a walking pace, trotting for only about a quarter of the time. Unfit horses should not be overworked; they must be brought into work gradually. It normally takes at least six weeks to get a horse fit. Overworking an unfit horse (particularly when young) is a frequent cause of lameness.

A really fit, properly fed horse is not easily overworked, provided certain conditions are observed. He must be considerately and intelligently ridden or driven, with a weight that is not too heavy and at a pace that is not too fast. Trotting at an excessive pace, particularly on hard surfaces, may cause strains and other injury through concussion. Trotting downhill also puts extra strain on the forelegs. In the case of riding horses, full use should be made of turf and other "soft going", avoiding cantering or galloping on hard ground. The legs can also be saved considerable strain by changing diagonals at the trot, that is, bumping once in the saddle and rising as the other foreleg comes to the ground.

When exercise lasts for more than two hours, during hunting for example, wherever possible the horse should be given 10–15 minutes rest – dismounting and slackening the girth, if possible. Long-distance endurance rides put great strain on a horse's constitution. Fluid and electrolyte losses from prolonged exercise and sweat loss can cause serious problems unless these are replaced. Anyone undertaking this sort of riding should seek veterinary advice about the supplements which are necessary to overcome these difficulties.

N.B. In addition to adjusting the girth soon after mounting, it should be rechecked during long periods of exercise, when it may also be necessary to tighten it.

Leading on Foot. Although a halter or head-collar can be used, a bridle always gives much greater control. When using a bridle, the reins must be taken over the animal's head – it should not be led with the reins over its neck. A horse is normally led from the near (left) side, the person leading it walking level and close to its head, holding the reins or rope in their right hand, close to the bit. These should be held firmly, but not so tightly as to interfere with the natural movement of the head. The end of the reins or rope should be held in the left hand, but never twisted round it. This will allow a little give and take when needed. A useful tip, if the horse plays up, is to press the right forearm firmly against its neck, at the same time tensing the wrist; in which way more control is possible.

If it should be necessary to lead a horse in a double bridle, the snaffle rein (bridoon bit) only should be used – the curb rein being tied at the neck.

A bridle must always be used when leading a horse on the road – even if the animal is one which is usually quiet and reliable. On the road, a horse must be led from the opposite side – from its off (right) – holding the reins in the left hand, so as to place the person leading it between the horse and the traffic.

Leading when Riding. A bridle must be used for the horse being led, and the reins passed over its head. If a martingale is fitted, this must be securely tied up and free of the reins. Whether both reins are held in one hand, or one pair in each hand, will depend on the rider's preference and the temperament of the horses. The reins of the led horse should not be looped round the fingers, but should be allowed to slip through them if the horse becomes troublesome or runs back. On the road, the led horse should be on the inside (left) and alongside the ridden one.

The Rule of the Road. The Highway Code says that you should keep to the left when riding. You should also keep to the left while leading a horse, on foot or while leading another. In a one-way street you should proceed only in the direction of the traffic, keeping to the left as much as possible.

If you are riding after sunset (which is not advised), the Highway Code says that you should wear light-coloured or reflective clothing, and carry lights which show white to the front and red to the rear.

At all times riders are expected to use their judgment to avoid accidents, and occasionally this might necessitate taking a horse to the opposite side of the road from usual. Responsibility would rest with the rider if an accident was caused through failure to do this.

A horse-drawn vehicle, like any other vehicle, should always keep well in to the left.

Strictly speaking, it is illegal to drive, ride or lead a horse on any footpath or other pedestrian right of way, though in practice it is often necessary to use these to pass in safety along busy roads.

Riders do have certain rights as road users and it is as well to know them:

Motorists are expected to slow down or stop if asked or when signalled to do so by any person in charge of horses. When they do, please remember to acknowledge the courtesy.

It is the law that a motorist concerned in an accident causing injury to a "domestic animal" (this term legally includes all farm animals and dogs, but, for some unexplained reason, excludes poultry and cats) must stop and, on request, give the number of his vehicle, his own name and address and those of the owner of the vehicle. If he does not do this at the time, he is required to report the accident to a Police Station or Constable within 24 hours.

Broadly speaking, the rules of the road are a matter of commonsense, combined with consideration for others, and if they were observed by all, with a little courtesy added, our roads would be pleasanter to travel.

Loading and Travelling. The problem of getting a horse into a horse-box is occasionally difficult, often leading to considerable excitement, loss of temper and accidents. In the majority of cases there would be less trouble if the task were tackled quietly and as a perfectly normal procedure, horses being quick to sense "an atmosphere". The ramp of the horse box must be lowered and everything ready before the horse is brought to it, otherwise the unusual sights and sounds are certain to arouse misgivings in his mind. Take the further precaution of spreading a small quantity of straw over the ramp to reassure the animal with something familiar under his feet. The ramps of horseboxes are provided with slats for foothold, but if necessary, ashes can be scattered on them for additional safety. If he is now led straight in without fuss as though into his own loose-box, there will probably be no resistance.

Unfortunately, the operation is not always so simple, however tactfully one approaches it, and one has to resort to guile or even force. When two horses are to be boxed, one that is known to be quiet should be led in first and the other may follow with confidence. If this fails, his stomach may over-rule his scruples if a feed or a hay-net are enticingly indicated inside the box. Even this does not always succeed, and one must prepare for trouble.

If a horse is reluctant to load, it is worthwhile taking time and trouble to get him accustomed to loading. This may entail persuading him to enter the horse-box or trailer and feeding him there on several occasions before the day on which he is to travel. If a horse will not load, and guile fails, it may be necessary to use additional persuasion. By lifting one foreleg up at a time, it may be possible to manoeuvre him up the ramp. Two people using a lungeing rein, or linking hands around the gaskins, may be able to propel the horse forward. If single-handed, fixing one end of a lungeing rein to the trailer, passing it round the back of the horse and holding the end, may encourage the horse forward sufficiently to load. As a last resort, a blindfold may be used, but care must be taken that the animal does not injure itself by stepping off the side of the ramp.

When travelling, consideration must be given to protecting the horse from injury. Travelling bandages over cotton wool or foam rubber will give protection to the legs. These must be applied down to the coronet, to protect against tread injuries. If a horse is a bad traveller and prone to injury, rubber coronet boots may provide additional protection. Injury to the tail is quite a common injury associated with travel, and fitting a tail bandage should be a routine measure. Care must be taken that these are not fitted too tightly or left on too long; they should never be left on overnight. If an animal is very fractious when travelling, a padded hood may prevent head injuries.

A hay-net should always be provided to keep a horse quiet and happy when travelling. On longer journeys (3 or 4 hours or more), it will be necessary to stop and offer water to the horse.

Fire in the Stable. Although every sensible person takes all possible steps to guard against fire, by strictly banning smoking, the striking of matches, etc., in the stable, one must be prepared for unavoidable accidents.

In the event of an outbreak, the first action is to get the

horses out as quickly as possible, naturally. Horses are particularly terrified of fire and quickly lose their heads, so that even the normally quiet, sensible animal may become stupid and difficult to handle. Although so terrified, it is not uncommon for a horse to refuse to leave a burning stable. If this happens, blindfold him, or better, cover his eyes and nostrils with a damp towel or sack and lead him out. Try backing him out if he is still obstinate. Cases have occurred, in large stables, of there being insufficent people to deal with the number of horses, and then all that can be done is to give every animal a chance to escape by throwing open the doors, concentrating the attention on those that refuse to leave. In such a case, waste no time in undoing head-ropes of tied horses. Unless quick-release knots have been used, simply cut the ropes and set them free as quickly as possible. Care must be taken that, once rescued, a horse does not break away back to the stable.

Now is the time, above all others, to keep calm, dealing quickly and efficiently but *quietly* with the task on hand. If there is any losing of heads to be done, the horses may be relied upon for this.

6

BEDDING

Horses are bedded down, primarily, to encourage them to lie down and rest. They can rest standing and, of course, there are horses which seldom lie down, but their condition is improved and the life of their legs increased by taking proper rest.

Inadequate bedding is almost as bad as none and is certainly false economy. A thin bed is quickly scraped away in places leaving the bare, hard floor exposed, from contact with which the elbows, fetlock joints and other parts are liable to injury, giving rise to such things as capped hock and capped elbow. Also there will be an unnecessarily wet and dirty horse to be groomed in the morning.

There are various materials that may be used for bedding, straw (of which there are several kinds), wood shavings, sawdust, peat moss, and shredded paper. Sand, leaves and bracken are not satisfactory bedding materials for horses, although they have been used for this purpose in the past.

Traditionally, wheat straw has been recommended as being the best bedding material for horses – the long hard straws making a good firm bed. Nowadays, barley straw is much more widely available and makes a perfectly acceptable bedding material. Modern methods of harvesting remove the awns which can cause skin irritation, thus removing the main reason why this type of straw was not recommended in the past. Oat straw is not usually used for bedding because, being very palatable, horses tend to eat it.

Shavings are often used for bedding. This material is especially useful for those animals that eat straw bedding. Shavings can be used fresh, or as deep litter bedding. Droppings and soiled material must be removed several times a day to keep a clean dry bed for the horse, and to prevent foot problems (especially thrush). Clean shavings are then added to the bed which should be raked to provide an even covering (ideally about 10cm (4″) deep).

The Shire

Sawdust is also sometimes used for bedding. It is not very absorbent and becomes heated when damp, so is not as satisfactory as shavings. Again, regular removal of droppings and soiled material is important.

Peat moss is another good form of bedding, though rather expensive. A depth of 20cm (8″) is needed, and this makes a good form of deep litter bedding if droppings and soiled material are removed regularly. However, it is not so easy to spot soiled material in this type of bedding. Rolling the surface, once the bed has been laid and raked level, can help prevent the horse churning it up.

Shredded paper is another satisfactory alternative bedding

which is particularly useful for horses that suffer from allergy to moulds in other forms of bedding.

Bedding down with Straw. Your aim in bedding down with straw will be to provide a warm level, elastic yet firm bed which will drain away moisture, provide protection against floor draughts and prevent injury from hard surfaces. If these points are remembered you will not go wrong.

Shake out the straw thoroughly when laying it, and, starting from the edges of the box, toss it so that it lies evenly over the floor with the straws crossing in different directions. If it is thrown down in lumps and with the straws lying parallel, it is less elastic and is soon dragged around by the horse's feet, leaving bare or thin patches. Push the bed well up against the sides and back of the box to give a saucer effect, which will be protection against draughts or injury from the walls. Banking the straw round the walls also helps to prevent the horse getting cast (stuck against the walls and unable to get up). At the front, by the door, leave a bare space if the floor is above the level of the ground outside, as it should be. This "doorstep" avoids an untidy appearance and is a "mind the step" notice to the horse when going in or out of the box. Finish the edge off by turning the straggling edges under neatly.

When using old and new bedding together, mix the two well before bedding down. Remember a good thick bed is an economy; apart from the comfort of the horse there will be less wastage and it will be so much easier to muck-out in the morning.

A common trouble with all types of straw, even wheat, is that of its being eaten by the horse. Many and varied are the remedies suggested – some say it is because the horse does not get sufficient hay, others advise tying him up as though he were in a stall – but still many horses turn to their bedding as an extra course. From experience, sprinkling the bed with Jeyes, or some other safe disinfectant, has usually been found effective in checking the habit. Time will show how much must be sprinkled. With animals which, however, look upon a dash of disinfectant as a condiment, I have found spraying the bed with fly-spray provides the answer.

Bedding down with Shavings, Sawdust, Peat Moss and Shredded Paper. Firstly, the entrance to the drains should be stopped up to prevent their becoming blocked. Secondly, the bedding must receive constant attention – remember that this bed is always down, unlike straw which can be completely removed for part of the day. Droppings must be removed even more frequently than is often the case with straw litter. Wet patches, likewise, must be taken out regularly and the place covered with fresh material. Lastly, even stricter attention must be paid to cleanliness of the horse's feet.

One of the most important causes of equine ill-health is an allergy to the spores of moulds and fungi in the stable environment. Hay is the most obvious source of spores, but bedding can be equally to blame. These spores are responsible for a lung condition which produces a harsh dry cough – a complaint that used to be called 'broken wind', but is now known as Chronic Obstructive Pulmonary Disease (or COPD). Many horses suffer from this problem, and it is worthwhile taking every possible precaution to reduce spores and stable dust to a minimum.

Straw, even when fresh and of good quality, contains large numbers of fungal spores. When the straw is of poor quality (fusty) or is used in deep litter bedding, spore levels in the stable may be very high. When used fresh, paper, shavings, sawdust, and peat have low levels of spores, but in deep litter situations they have little advantage over straw. Stable ventilation is particularly important in keeping the dust to an acceptable level. If ventilation is inadequate, even good quality straw may lead to potentially damaging levels of spores in the stable atmosphere. Spore levels are at their highest when bedding is being shaken up, so it is always advisable to do this when the horse is not in the stable – allowing 20 minutes for the dust to settle before the horse is returned to its box. A regime for minimising spores (including soaking hay or replacing it with some other form of fibre; using fresh shavings or paper bedding, and so on) is essential for any horse that suffers from COPD. Even when horses do not show signs of this problem, it is still a wise precaution to try and keep spore levels in the stable to a low level to avoid sensitising them and producing the problem in the future.

MUCKING-OUT

"Mucking-out" is the very appropriate term applied to the early morning cleaning of the stables.

Having already mentioned the attention required by peat moss litter and similar forms of bedding, it only remains to deal with straw. The task is simple enough – the separation of the clean from the wet, dirty bedding and droppings – but requires some practice. Using the "stable fork", the clean straw is removed first to a convenient corner and then, in the interests of economy, that which is not too wet or dirty to be used again is shaken from the remainder and follows the clean. Now the short and the dirty stuff, together with the droppings, are swept up, loaded on to a wheelbarrow and carted away to the manure heap. This heap adorns a corner of the premises not near enough to be unpleasant or attract flies and not so far away as to necessitate a long journey; a brick enclosure is ideal for storing manure. Making a good square manure heap assists rotting down of the material. This takes up less space and also helps to reduce flies – the heat of well rotted manure kills developing flies. Treating the outer less rotted material with an insecticidal spray, during the summer, will further reduce the fly problem.

Regularly and frequently the floor should be washed down with plenty of water plus disinfectant, special attention being given to the corners, and the drains sluiced out. While horses are out, keep all windows and doors wide open to air the place completely. In summer, spraying with a good proprietary fluid helps to keep down flies and other insects and makes the stable healthy and pleasant.

7

GROOMING

To understand the reasons for grooming it is necessary to know something about the skin and the coat.

There are two skins, the most sensitive "dermis", containing the roots of the hair, the sweat and oil glands, blood vessels and nerves; protecting the dermis is the dry, insensitive "epidermis", which is constantly being shed in the form of scurf. The purpose of sweating is to keep the body temperature level, and, through the pores, to throw off some of its waste products. The coat, providing warmth and protection, is greased and waterproofed by the oil glands.

In domestication, the horse works harder and faster, consuming more heat-producing foods than in its natural state, so that the skin and the sweat glands are called upon to function more actively. To enable them to carry out their work efficiently, the skin must be kept clean by grooming, and the sweat glands stimulated by massage. Cleanliness is also a preventive of skin diseases which are encouraged to spread by dirty conditions, whilst massage assists in toning up the muscles.

In attaining these objectives, the final purpose of grooming is automatically achieved – appearance.

GROOMING KIT

There are certain tools used for the various operations of grooming:

Hoof Pick. The hoof pick is a blunt hook used for removing dirt and stones from the feet. When used, it is not forced down the side or cleft of the frog harder than necessary, and is worked from the heel to the toe.

Dandy Brush. The dandy brush is usually of stiff whisk fibre and is employed for the removal of hard, caked dirt from the coat, particularly on the legs.

Body Brush and Curry Comb. These are always used together. The brush, of short, stout bristles, with a loop of webbing across the back to keep it on the hand, is for removing scurf and dirt. There are two types of Curry Comb, the handiest being the "Cavalry" pattern, which consists of a metal plate with several blunt-toothed blades on one side and a webbing loop on the other for securing it to the *back* of the hand. The other type is the "Jockey", which is fitted with a wooden handle instead of the hand loop. The advantage of the first is that the palm of the hand on which it is secured is left free and can be placed on the horse during grooming. The purpose of the curry comb is primarily for cleaning the body brush of collected scurf; an occasional rub is given on the brush and the side of the comb is knocked on the floor. It is, however, effective used on the horse for the removal of dried mud with which the dandy brush is unable to deal.

Water Brush. The water brush is a very gentle one, with softer and longer bristles than the others, and in addition to its purpose of damping the mane and tail, and washing the legs and feet (when really necessary), is excellent for grooming the head and face which are too sensitive for stiffer brushes.

Sponges and Stable Rubber. A sponge is normally used for cleaning the eyes, lips and nostrils – a separate one being kept for cleaning the dock. The stable rubber is a cloth which is used for giving the coat a final polish after grooming.

Mane and Tail Comb. This is, or should be, rarely needed. It is made of light metal and has broad teeth. This comb should be used as little as possible in actual grooming as it is very liable to do more harm than good, by breaking or tearing out the hair. It may be found necessary in such operations as plaiting the mane, "pulling" the mane and tail, or trimming leg feathering, all of which are described in Chapter 8.

Sweat Scraper. This is a curved metal or rubber strip attached to a handle which can, as the name suggests, be used to scrape the lather off a horse which has been sweating excessively. It may also be used to remove water from the coat when, for any reason, it has been necessary to wash it. It is, however, far better that your horse should not be allowed to get into the state where a sweat scraper is required.

Wisp. This is a twisted rope of hay or straw, 2.5 metres (8 ft) long, with two loops at one end, one slightly longer than the other. The rope is plaited around each loop in turn and secured at the end in one of the twists. When dampened, a wisp is an ideal means of massage, helping to develop and harden muscles, but also producing a shine on the coat.

METHOD OF GROOMING

Perhaps the best way of describing the method of grooming will be to deal with it as it occurs in the daily routine.

Quartering. Before exercising it is desirable to "quarter". This is merely a quick light grooming to make the horse presentable. In this, as in all grooming operations, start by picking out the feet, as already described. Follow this by brushing off all stable marks with the dandy; if the horse has been properly bedded down the previous evening, these marks will be few and dry. Then, with the body brush, quickly brush down the mane and tail. The head and face can be rubbed over, and the eyes, nose, lips and dock sponged. The whole operation should take only five or ten minutes.

Cooling and Drying Off. On returning from exercise the horse should, ordinarily, be cool and dry, having been walked and allowed to cool off after work. However, if the horse is wet or sweating it must be dried off on its return to the stable. When wet from rain, wisping with loose straw, followed by the rubber, will get the horse dry and warm. Particular attention must be paid to the heels and the backs of the pasterns, which must be dried to prevent cracked heels developing. If the horse has been worked hard and for a long period, it helps to massage the back muscles under the saddle to restore circulation. If the

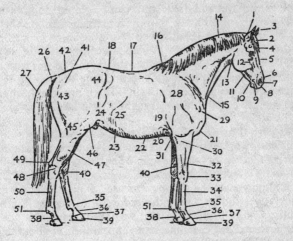

KEY TO POINTS OF THE HORSE

Head and Neck
1. Poll (Nape of Neck
2. Forelock
3. Ears
4. Forehead
5. Face
6. Muzzle
7. Nostrils
8. Upper Lip
9. Lower Lip
10. Chin Groove
11. Lower Jaw
12. Cheekbone
13. Jowl
14. Mane (Crest)
15. Throat (Windpipe)

Trunk or Body
16. Withers
17. Back
18. Loins
19. Side of Chest
20. Girth Place
21. Breast (Chest)
22. Floor of Chest
23. Belly
24. Flank
25. Barrel

Tail
26. Dock (Root of Tail)
27. Hair of Tail

Limbs and Croup
28. Shoulder
29. Point of Shoulder
30. Arm (True Arm)
31. Elbow
32. Forearm
33. Knee
34. Cannon (Shank) Bone
35. Fetlock Joint
36. Pastern
37. Coronet
38. Heel
39. Hoof
40. Chestnut
41. Haunch
42. Croup
43. Hip Joint
44. Point of Hip
45. Upper Thigh
46. Stifle
47. Lower Thigh
48. Hock
49. Point of Hock
50. Flexor Tendons
51. Feathering (in heavy horses)

Fig. 3   Points of the Horse

horse is very wet and tired, straw can be placed along its back and quarters, under a rug, to provide extra insulation to help it dry off and prevent a chill. When drying the horse do not forget to dry the head, especially the ears. Occasionally, a horse will break out in a sweat again after drying off. In this case, the horse will have to be dried off a second time, and will probably require rugging up to prevent a chill. This is one reason why it is necessary to check a horse at night after a hard day's work.

Strapping. Having taken the necessary precautions after exercise or work, you will start your real grooming or strapping with the horse dry and cool. When properly carried out, grooming is a very tiring business when one is unused to it, the chief requirement being "elbow grease". It must be performed quickly, yet thoroughly and vigorously, to achieve the best results; a horse in the condition we have in mind now can be well groomed, for cleanliness and appearance, in about thirty minutes. Further time spent, particularly with the wisp, will help to put muscle on both animal and groom.

Do not forget to get busy, first, with the hoof pick. Then, with a dandy brush, begin at the neck just behind the ear and thoroughly brush out the coat, the way the hair lies, to remove sweat marks and dried mud. It is well to point out here that mud should be left to dry before an attempt is made to brush it off. It may be washed off before it dries, but if this is done the skin must be thoroughly dried afterwards with sawdust, straw, etc., or chapping of the skin will result – causing cracked heels. This is a common problem in winter. At this time of year repeated washing is not advisable as it removes the protective oils from the skin; it is much better to let mud dry and then brush it off.

After the dandy brush comes the real work with the body brush, getting right through the coat and clearing scurf and dried sweat from the skin itself. It is customary to begin on the near side, that is, the horse's left, when for the most part the brush will be on the left hand and the curry comb on the right; on the offside the brush will be on the right hand and the curry comb on the left. In this way more force can be used behind the brush. Take your stand, with the feet apart, a little away from the horse so that weight can be put on the brush to drive the bristles through the coat, steadying yourself with the right hand on the horse. Remember to scrape the body brush across the curry comb periodically during grooming, to remove scurf and dust, but do not put more work into cleaning the brush than you do into cleaning the horse. With a vigorous circular motion, work down the neck and along the body, not forgetting the part between the forelegs and the belly, finishing by using the brush in the direction of the coat. Now turn your attention to the near legs, not neglecting the inside of the thighs. When grooming the hindlegs, particularly on the inside, grasp the hamstring with the free hand; it may be a ticklish spot you are dealing with now and the hold on the hamstring is a guard against kicks. Many grooms prefer to brush the inside of the opposite legs while on the near side and do the inside of the near legs when working on the offside. Now repeat the whole process on the other side.

Cob

By this time, if you have been grooming properly, you should feel as if you had been doing some hard work. However, the next item is one which must be dealt with gently. For the head it is much better to use the water brush, even the body brush may be too severe for this sensitive part. Do not forget the ears, brush them out against the palm of the hand, the tip of the ear held under the thumb.

The mane comes next, and here you should use the body brush, as the dandy is inclined to pull and break the hair. Here, as elsewhere, scurf must be removed from the *roots*. First brush the mane out to clear any tangles – do not use the mane comb for this purpose unless the mane is very thick. Then brush out lock by lock for cleanliness and finally straight down. A well-kept mane enhances a horse's appearance.

Now clean the eyes, nostrils, lips and dock, in that order, with damp sponges, or cloths, and remember to wash them thoroughly afterwards.

The tail should be dealt with in a similar fashion to the mane. The subject of tail-pulling and bandaging is discussed in the Chapters "Clipping and Trimming" (page 61) and "Clothing" (page 68), but all that is necessary now is to get the hair clean and lying down smoothly. A damp water brush will help to make the hair at the root tidy.

To put the finishing touches to the grooming operations, give the coat a final polish with the stable rubber – a chamois leather is excellent for this.

Your horse should now be clean and smart, but, unless time is limited, before using the rubber, put in some work with the wisp. This is slapped down smartly on the coat in the direction of the hair but is not used on the head, loins, or any delicate, sensitive parts. A quick wisping again in the evening is beneficial.

Washing Horses. Washing horses is not a normal practice in the U.K. although in warmer climates it can safely be carried out. Washing removes the natural oils from the coat which are needed by the animal to protect it from the weather. In the U.K., washing should be limited to removing stains on grey or other light-coloured horses, and to the mane and tail, when necessary. A shampoo recommended for animal use should be used for this purpose, not domestic detergents. In the summer, a horse may be washed before a show, but at other times of the year it should not be done.

8

CLIPPING AND TRIMMING

Reasons for Clipping. In winter, the horse grows a thicker and longer coat for protection and as some compensation for the decreased quality and quantity of food available in natural conditions. Under domestication, the necessary food is supplied (or should be) by man, but protection against cold is still required and nature continues to provide the winter coat, which makes its appearance in the autumn and is shed again in the spring.

For a horse living out at grass, the extra covering, and its additional grease, are essential. Taking no more exercise than necessary, or than he feels inclined to, no body heat is lost, nor discomfort suffered, from sweating. For a stabled and working animal, however, a thick coat has many disadvantages. None of us would care to perform hard physical work while dressed in a fur coat; we would perspire freely and tire quickly. So it is with a horse; he cannot be expected to work thus and keep condition. Satisfactory grooming is difficult, with the result that the pores become clogged with waste products which cannot be properly cleared from the skin. Drying after work, and possibly a soaking with rain or snow, is even more difficult and laborious, and chills follow. All these troubles are overcome by clipping.

When not working, a clipped horse must be compensated for the loss of his coat by clothing, or chills again are invited. Clothing takes the form of "rugs", varying in number according to the temperature. Types of clothing are dealt with in Chapter 9, (page 63).

Times for Clipping. In a normal year, the winter coat is usually well-established in October or November, and the first clipping can take place then, followed by a second early in the New Year. The theory that clipping after the New Year spoils the summer coat is unfounded, and although twice is sometimes sufficient, the clippers may be used whenever the hair grows noticeable. Directly the summer coat shows signs of coming through in the spring (probably April or May) there should be no more clipping, but it is seldom that it need continue far into the year. The coat reacts quickly to changes in temperature, and the dates for first and last clipping can only be decided by weather conditions.

Types of Clip. There are five types of clip, to suit different purposes:

For a horse or pony doing light work at slow paces, either a *Full Trace Clip* or a *Small Trace Clip* is used. The hair is removed from the belly and the upper parts of the legs (from the middle of the forearm and gaskins to approximately the trace height of a cart harness, level with the point of the shoulders) and the mane and tail are left. In many cases, the hair on the underside of the neck and face is also clipped out.

For a horse that is doing light work, a *Blanket Clip* is used. The hair is removed only from the neck and belly; a patch corresponding in size to that of a horse blanket is left on the body. This clip makes it easier to keep the horse clean, but avoids the need to keep the horse rugged up all the time. It can be useful when the horse spends part of the day turned out.

For a fit horse doing hard work in winter, it is usual to clip it right out, down to the ground – a *Full Clip*. As the name indicates, the whole body, legs and head, are clipped, leaving only the tail, mane and forelock – unless that is already "hogged", that is, clipped short.

The *Hunter Clip* is a variation of the Full Clip, the difference being that the legs are only partly clipped, as in the Trace Clip, and a "saddle-patch" is left on the back by clipping around the saddle. It is a common practice to clip right out the first time and to adopt the Hunter Clip subsequently in the New Year, especially for fine-coated animals.

As there is controversy as to the merits of the Hunter Clip, the arguments for and against are set out on page 57:

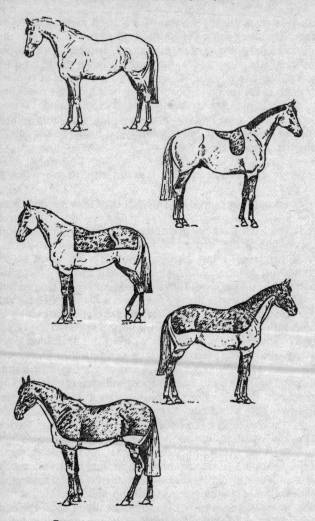

From top to bottom: Full Clip, Hunter Clip,
Blanket Clip, Full Trace Clip, Small Trace
Clip.

Fig. 4   Types of Clip

For leaving the legs:
(a) Protection from cold and from thorns, etc.
(b) The hair on the back of the fetlock joints acts as a drain for sweat and wet, preventing cracked heels (chapping) by keeping them dry.

Against:
(a) It does not afford *complete* protection from thorns, and when these are picked up they are more easily detected and removed without the hindrance of long hair.
(b) There is little force in the "drain" reasoning, since unclipped horses at grass sometimes suffer from cracked heels, and in a stabled horse, the legs, clipped or not, must be dried on return from work if they are wet, the task being more difficult with long, thick hair; in any case a small tuft could be left at the back of the joint to act as a drain.

For a saddle-patch:
(a) Saddle galls are prevented.
(b) Short hairs left after complete clipping may be a source of irritation if forced into the back by the rider's weight.
(c) A cold saddle on a clipped back is disliked and may cause bucking.

Against:
(a) How can the coat prevent galling, since saddle injuries are caused by friction due to loose girthing or bad riding, or by pressure from an ill-fitting saddle on parts unprotected by muscle?
(b) The point about irritation from short "stump" hairs, reasonable in theory, is unsupported in practice – at least to any appreciable extent.
(c) The objection to a cold saddle can be overcome by saddling up loosely a few minutes before mounting, as should always be done with any horse.
(d) A saddle patch causes considerable sweating of the back and there is danger of chills if it is not properly dried; drying the back is extra work avoided by clipping.

In summary, whether a Full Clip or a Hunter Clip is used is a matter of personal preference.

Clipping Equipment. Though hand clippers can be used for "hogging" a mane or trimming the hair around fetlocks, electric clippers are used for clipping the body hair. It is important that the blades are sharp and the equipment is well maintained; damaged blades, which may cut the horse, should not be used. When buying clippers, it is worthwhile selecting a model which makes the least noise, to reduce to a minimum the risk of frightening the animal.

The Operation. Choose a mild day for clipping; a cold, blustery spell is no time for depriving the horse of his natural overcoat, and, of course, do not clip if he has a cold or is in any other way "off colour". Even though you will be rugging up afterwards, he needs a little time to become acclimatised. Be sure everything is in order for going straight through with operations without any hitch; clippers must be sharp, and cleaned and oiled at intervals during clipping. Blunt blades make hard work and indifferent results, and by pulling on the horse's hair, are more inclined to upset it. Have the horse thoroughly clean or the clippers will soon be blunted. There must be sufficient time to finish the job without a last-minute rush.

Many horses are apprehensive about being clipped and a few animals violently object. Always begin quietly, treating the horse as perfectly normal, only using methods of restraint when absolutely necessary. A bridle gives better control and should be used unless the horse is exceptionally quiet. A few horses will need to be "twitched" in order to clip them. (A "twitch" distracts the horse's attention from an unpleasant operation, by applying pressure on the muzzle – which is a very sensitive part. It consists of a round stick (broomstick or axe handle) about 50–60cm (18–24") long, with a piece of rope threaded through a hole in the end. The rope is formed into a loop large enough to admit the fist, placed on the upper lip and tip of the nose, and the stick given a turn or two. It should be left on no longer than necessary, and the nose should be rubbed to restore circulation after it has been removed.) A "twitch" can be useful when clipping ticklish areas of the body on an otherwise quiet horse. If, however, an animal violently objects to being clipped, it is best to call the vet to give it a sedative injection. Modern tranquillising drugs for horses are very effective and by their use, even the more awkward horse can normally be made quiet enough to clip without risk to horse or operator.

Where you start on a horse is a matter of choice. Some begin at the neck, others prefer the hindquarters, but the head is usually left to the last. First get the blades moving steadily, then apply them to the coat against the lay of the hair, with an even pressure to avoid a ridgy effect. Very little practice is required to take the coat off evenly on the broader expanses, but at "corners" and the angle of bones some skill is called for; loose skin, such as at the junction of the elbows with the body, should be pulled flat. At the crest, take care not to run up into the mane, edge the coat off gradually to leave a smooth finish – this is particularly necessary when the mane is not "hogged". Where the tail joins the body, at the top, leave a small "V", pointing forward, to give a neat effect. In the head, the bones are near the surface and you must work with care – watch also the root of the forelock, do not go too far and cut the long hair.

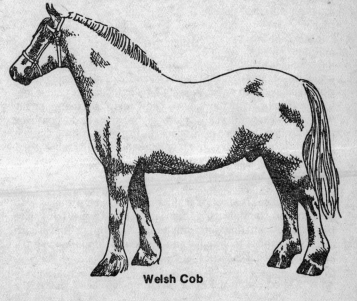

Welsh Cob

You will notice "feelers" or whiskers on the muzzle; many people take these off to save themselves trouble, but *they must be left*, and the skilful person clips carefully around them. The ears you can deal with easily by holding them *flat* in your free hand and running the blades downwards from their tips; do not clip inside, fold them together and run the clippers along the edges.

In the Trace Clips and Hunter Clip, slant the boundary line of the hair that is being left, upwards and forwards. For neatness, lightly trim the long feathering at the backs of the legs, edging off the hair around so that no obvious ridge is left. To leave a saddle patch in the Hunter Clip, your horse must be saddled up to mark the boundary. Having clipped around the saddle to get the correct shape, take it off and cut your patch a little smaller so that it will not show when the horse is saddled.

Operations completed, brush the horse down and rug up immediately – in fact it is advisable to throw a rug over when the body is finished. For a few days after, increase the food ration slightly and allow more bedding to compensate for loss of warmth.

TRIMMING

Trimming can be defined as the process of making a horse's appearance smarter and neater, and approximating more nearly to one with more "quality", by reducing the coarse hair and feathering. It includes, also, "tidying up" the mane and tail when these grow unevenly or straggly. Scissors and a comb are generally used in place of clippers, and long or unwanted hair is pulled out by hand. It is an art which calls for skill and practice, and great care must be exercised, especially in early attempts, or the result will be worse.

Legs. Long, coarse hair or feathering should be trimmed with scissors and comb, leaving them smooth and even. To achieve this, it is better to take your time and remove only a little at each cut – you cannot replace hair and it takes a long time to grow and cover mistakes.

Mane. On occasions the mane has to be "levelled", that is, the hair which grows down beyond the general length and gives it an untidy appearance, has to be pulled out – a few hairs only at a time.

It is rarely necessary to "hog" the mane, and it is good to note that this is less frequently done now. A few horses may look better without their manes, such as those which grow only a poor, short one, but often its removal discloses or accentuates a "ewe neck" which was better hidden. (A "ewe neck" is one shaped like a sheep's, curving downwards in the middle.) For "hogging", hand clippers are used, care being taken not to leave a sharp dividing line where the hair of the neck is met.

Keeping the mane all on one side (custom says the offside) is really a matter of grooming, when a damped water brush is usually sufficient to "lay" it. Stubborn manes, however, may be "laid" by plaiting. In the stable it obviously does not matter how many plaits you make, but when dressing up for the show ring it is "not done" to have more than six. They should not be left in for more than a day at a time or there will be a tendency for the hair to break. When it is unplaited, brush out the mane well and get the curls out.

Tail. The clippers are never used on the tail. If it is desired to level the end, use scissors or special tail shears. The length is largely a matter of taste and from the horse's point of view, the longer the better, but many people like it shortened ("banged") to a hand's breadth below the points of the hocks when the horse is moving – at which time it is lifted slightly. To cut the tail, raise it to judge the required length, then, with a second person holding it with a hand either side of the place chosen, cut so that there is a very slight downward and backward slope, that is, the hair nearest the horse is a little shorter than on the outside.

"Pulling" the tail, or making it neat and tidy at the root, must be carried out a little at a time to avoid soreness, a few hairs from the lower part being removed at each pull, and any long hairs from the sides. (Do not interfere with the hairs on the outer surface and never cut the tail near the root, or a bristly effect will result.) This is frequently hard on the fingers, which may become cut in the process, so a mane comb can be used, the hair being twisted into the teeth. Tail-pulling is a fetish with many people and one often sees horses with tails almost naked half-way down the dock, but sensibly carried out it does make a great improvement in appearance. However, if you do not feel equal to the task, good grooming does much to keep a tail tidy, and your horse will be none the worse – probably far happier. Remember, too, a horse living out needs all the protection from weather that he can get, and which a bushy tail provides for the delicate parts beneath. The tail is also a horse's only protection from flies. By shortening it unnecessarily, you are depriving it of its most effective means of defence against attacks by these insects in summer months.

In the horse world, even yet, there is too much care and thought bestowed on custom, tradition and appearance, and not enough on the animal itself. Keep your horse fit and well by good feeding, grooming and general management and his appearance will be a source of pride without any beauty parlour treatment.

9

CLOTHING

For all normal stable purposes, a stable rug is all that is necessary in the way of clothing for the clipped horse. In severe weather, two can be used at a time, or alternatively a horse blanket placed underneath one. For horses kept out all the year round, a waterproof, canvas-covered "New Zealand" Rug is invaluable for fine-coated animals or others which cannot withstand the winter climate. Although "New Zealand" Rugs are sometimes recommended for clipped horses living out, the wisdom of clipping any horse that must "winter out" is highly questionable, unless a minimal Trace Clip is used.

Night Rugs. Traditionally, these are made of jute with a woollen lining, but modern quilted man-made fabrics are much more commonly used today. A Night Rug extends from the root of the tail to the withers, then downward and forward around the base of the neck, meeting at the middle of the breast, and reaches down to the level of the elbows. Three stock sizes are usual: "Pony" (up to 14 h.h.), "Cob" (14-15 h.h.) and "Hunter" (above 15 h.h.). It is shaped to the contours of the body, that is, with allowance for the rise at the withers and quarters. There is a leather, webbing or nylon strap fastened to a buckle at the breast. To prevent the rug slipping sideways, it usually has a surcingle attached. This is a broad webbing or nylon strap passing over the back at the withers, fastened on the near side by buckles. It is better, however, to have instead a separate "roller", a surcingle well padded where it crosses the spine, to obviate injury from pressure, and fitted with buckles and leather straps on the near side. With the former, it is advisable to place a thick, soft pad under the surcingle either side of the backbone, so shaped that this part is free from direct or indirect pressure. At the hindquarters there may be a braided cord (fillet string) passing round the buttocks from one rear corner of the rug to the other. Alternatively, some rugs have straps starting further forward, passing inside each thigh to fasten on the rear edge of the rug on the opposite site. The purpose of these straps is to prevent the corners from blowing up or being otherwise displaced.

Day Rugs. In practice, Night Rugs are often used in the daytime too, but it is helpful to have a separate Day Rug so that the Night Rug can be cleaned and aired. A thin, light rug of cotton ("Summer" or "Day Sheet") can be used for warm days and keeps the coat clean after grooming. A Sweat Rug, made of open cotton mesh, can also be useful for a hot horse returning from exercise. This enables the horse to cool off without catching a chill and can be replaced by the Night Rug when the horse is dry. Night Rugs of natural material can be placed over a Sweat Rug, but those made of man-made fibres may not allow the skin to "breathe".

Exercise Sheets. Smaller sheets are sometimes used during exercise. In winter, these may be of waterproof material and cover the shoulders and hindquarters. In summer, a light cotton sheet may be used.

Waterproof Rugs ("New Zealand" Rugs). These outdoor rugs are made of waterproofed canvas, lined with blanketing, and are more loosely fitting at the lower ("skirt") part than stable rugs, and allow freedom of movement. They buckle at the breast, in the same way, but strong leather straps with spring hooks take the place of fillet strings. They are made in the usual sizes: Pony, Cob, and Hunter.

It is claimed for these rugs that they afford sufficient protection from the weather, and that they right themselves after rolling. There is no doubt they are useful, but particular care is necessary in their fitting, and they should be adjusted frequently. As all rugs tend to slide back and the withers and shoulders soon become chafed; it is a wise precaution to pad them here. In the "New Zealand", since there is no surcingle, the leg straps have to be tight enough to keep it in place, and these must have frequent, generous treatment with neatsfoot oil, not only to preserve the leather but to keep it soft, the tender skin inside the thighs being especially liable to chafing. The surcingle on the All Weather rug must be inspected regularly to see that it has not tightened.

"Rugging Up". The right way to put on a rug is *not* to throw it on and then jiggle it straight. First fold it inside out, with the tail end up as far as the neck opening; then holding it at this part, the right hand taking the off, and the left the near side, gently throw it across the withers from the near side, further forward than it will be when fastened. Now buckle or tie at the breast and unfold the rug so that its centre line lies along the backbone; do not, even now, pull it back as far as it will go, leave the neck opening rather loose – in the way of all rugs it will slide back all too soon and tighten there. Before fastening the surcingle, make sure it lies flat; being out of sight, the offside has a sneaky way of twisting, and it will usually manage a double twist so that nothing is suspected. With a roller, loosely fold up the longer end, place the pad in position immediately behind the withers, push the folded end down on the offside, then bring it under the horse at the girth place and buckle on the near side. With both surcingle and roller, straighten out any wrinkles in the skirt of the rug after fastening, and do not buckle uncomfortably tightly – you should be able to run the fingers down, flat, between it and the rug to straighten it. Finally, tie the fillet strings – not tightly, but so that they hang in a loop reaching to just above halfway up the gaskins (except in the New Zealand).

Cleaning Rugs. When both Day and Night Rugs are used, one can be aired while the other is worn. In all cases, they should be shaken out and brushed on both sides when taken off. Night Rugs are particularly liable to soiling and it may be necessary to scrub them lightly – with the minimum of water – stretching while drying, to avoid shrinking.

Clothing being a frequent means of spreading skin diseases, each horse should have its own rugs which should not be used on other animals, even when apparently healthy. Ringworm spores can persist on clothing for long periods and can re-infect horses at a later date. Any clothing used on a horse that has had ringworn must be treated with a disinfectant that will kill fungi.

BANDAGES

The practice of bandaging is often abused in stables, and, as in many other matters, has become almost a convention with little regard to necessity. Whilst bandages are useful in certain circumstances, they can be harmful, especially when inexpertly applied. If too tight, they may not only interfere with the circulation but may actually cause serious damage to the tendons that they are supposed to be protecting and supporting. Excluding the surgical, the purposes of the three types in use – stable, working and tail – are discussed below.

Before any bandage is applied, it should be correctly rolled; tapes are attached at one end for fastening, and the bandages should be rolled tightly and evenly from here, with the tapes folded inside. Beginning on the outside of the limb, and pressing the end of the bandage against it with the left hand, pass the roll closely round the leg with the right until the starting point is reached; now the left hand, still holding the end in place, takes the roll while the right is brought back. From here onwards, the bandage is unrolled in a downward spiral, the left hand always holding in place the previous turn, which is overlapped by the next by about half its width. When the required distance has been covered, unroll in an upward spiral until the first turn is covered, then tie the tapes around the leg, finishing with a secure bow on the outside, and tucking in the ends. If tied on the inside it may be rubbed undone by the shoe of the opposite foot, and if tied on the tendon, may raise a lump. No turn should be tighter than the previous one, nor should the tapes be tighter than the bandage.

Stable and Travelling Bandages. These can be used for warmth during illness; as a covering for surgical bandages, to keep them clean and in position; and as a protection from injury when travelling in a box or trailer. Their use in cases of "filled" legs (that is, swollen, usually through inactivity) can scarcely be defended; the correct procedure with any complaint is to treat the cause, not the symptom.

Exmoor Pony

The bandages should be removed twice daily and the legs hand-rubbed to guard against interference with the circulation.

They are of wool, stockinet or a mixture of wool and cotton, and are about 2.5 metres (8 ft) in length and 10cm (4″) in width. Since they must not affect the circulation, they should not be put on any tighter than is necessary to keep them in place, and a layer of cotton wool or Gamgee tissues beneath is recommended, as a precaution against pressure and as additional warmth or protection. For travelling, pieces of foam are sometimes used under bandages to provide extra protection. Stable bandages should extend from immediately below the knee or hock, over the fetlock and pastern, to the coronet. It will be found impossible to make them lie smoothly over the pastern joint, but any loose folds here will be covered by the following turn.

Working Bandages. These can be used as protection for the legs and tendons during work where injury is likely – as in fast work and jumping – but are unneccessary for normal exercise. Good, sound tendons need no support in ordinary work. They should be left on no longer than they are needed.

Working Bandages are of stockinet, crepe, or other synthetic elastic material, and about 2 metres (6½ ft) in length and 8-10cm (3-4″) in width. Being elastic, and applied over cotton wool, they can be tighter than stable bandages, and should extend from just under the knee or hock to the fetlock joint without interfering with the movement of either. Because of the danger of the tapes being too tight or coming undone, the ends of the bandages are often stitched to hold them in place or, alternatively, secured by sticking plaster. Sufficient of the surplus cotton wool showing above and below the bandage should be pulled out to make the final effect neat, leaving about 1.5cm (½″) visible.

Tail Bandages. Although many horseowners spend time mastering the art of applying a tail bandage, the only time when this is really necessary is to protect the tail from rubbing, such as a horse that continually rubs its tail, or when travelling. Some serious injuries have occurred when tail bandages have been applied too tightly and left on for too long. As a rule, a tail bandage should not be left on longer than necessary, i.e. NOT overnight. Tail bandages are usually made of stockinet and should cover the dock (stopping just short of the last tail bone). The last two turns are carried over the first, around the root of the tail, the tapes finishing in a bow on top, with the ends tucked in. To remove, slide the whole off down the tail.

OTHER PROTECTIVE CLOTHING

Knee Caps. These are fitted to protect the knees from injury, particularly when doing roadwork in icy conditions or when a horse is known to stumble. They are made of felt and leather and have a padded upper strap which keeps the cap in place. The lower strap is loose to allow freedom of movement.

Hock Boots. These are similar to knee caps and used for protection. They can be useful when travelling, or for a horse that persists in kicking the walls of its stable.

Coronet Boots ("Over-reach" Boots). These are made of rubber and are fitted over the foot just around the pastern. They protect the heels and can be used at exercise in horses that have a tendency to over-reach. They are also helpful when fitted to travelling horses to protect the coronet from tread wounds (most often, travelling bandages would be used for this purpose).

Travelling Boots. Made of foam rubber, these may be used instead of travelling bandages. They are fitted from the knee and hock, down to the coronet, thus providing the protection of Knee Caps, Hock Boots and Travelling Bandages all in one.

Other Protective Boots. A variety of other boots are used to provide protection at exercise to the legs of horses which, because of some defect in their action, are prone to self-inflicted injury. Thus, *Fetlock Boots*, with a protective leather pad covering the inner part of the fetlock joints, may protect from "brushing" wounds. Injury from the hind leg to the inside of the foreleg (speedy cutting) may be prevented by *Speedy Cutting Boots,* while injury to the tendons can be prevented by *Tendon Boots.*

Great care must be taken when fitting all these boots to ensure that they do not come loose during exercise, and that they are not too tight. The straps and buckles are fitted on the outside of the leg, starting with the middle strap and working upwards and downwards.

10

TRICKS AND VICES

It is a fact that horses are seldom vicious by nature, but many become so due to bad treatment in one form or another. In some cases the trouble may be traced back to rough and unsympathetic handling by the breaker, in others to bad stable management, teasing, evidence of fear by those in charge, or, only too often, to downright ill-treatment.

What may be termed "bad habits" are frequently acquired, either during the early stages of training, in which case they prove difficult to cure, or later, in imitation of other horses. Nervousness and dubious temperament are traits which can be inherited. Horses possessing either of these tendencies are much more prone to develop stable vices and bad habits.

To cure these tricks and vices, many methods, both simple and complicated, have been devised and a few of the more simple ones will be mentioned here. It has been proved that the best results are obtained in all cases by good stable management and, above all, by sensible, sympathetic yet firm handling. Find, if you can, the cause of the trouble and then proceed, by commonsense means, to put things right and it is probable you will have no need to resort to the more drastic methods.

Biting. This, fortunately, is not a very common vice, although many horses will make playful snatches and nips on certain occasions. This is little to worry about, but may develop unpleasantly and should not be aggravated by teasing. Make allowances for ticklish spots and be gentle there, but at the same time firmly check any tendency towards nipping.

Ponies have a tendency towards nipping. This is often made much worse by feeding tit-bits – particularly if one animal only is being fed among a group at grass. Tit-bits should be stopped when any animal shows signs of nipping, and it is best not to give them at all to grazing animals.

Many stallions are natural biters and care should be taken walking past their boxes. It is for this reason that bars are sometimes placed across the top half of the stable door.

If you have a vicious biter to contend with, the sort that lays back his ears, shows the whites of his eyes and really tries to get you, it is probable that mere firm treatment will have little effect. There are several ways of dealing with an animal of this kind. For grooming, tying him up short so that he cannot reach you will be sufficient. Other ways are the use of the muzzle or the "side-stick". The side-stick is a stick of suitable thickness and length attached to the noseband of the headcollar and to the pad of a surcingle, to restrict movement. Both muzzle and side-stick must, of course, be removed for feeding, etc. or when not actually required.

There is one other means which not only checks biting but may also help to cure it. This is a snaffle bit of thick wood or hard rubber, which causes the horse a certain amount of pain when he bites on it.

Crib Biting and Windsucking. These two vices may, with advantage, be considered together and, in fact, they not infrequently accompany each other.

The crib biter grips with the teeth any available fitting, such as a manger, at the same time gulping down air, whilst the windsucker swallows air without gripping a fixed object. Thus it will be seen at once that attempting to cure crib-biting merely by removing all fittings may lead to windsucking. No permanent cure can be guaranteed for either complaint, but these vices can often be controlled (with varying degrees of success) by mechanical means. In cases where the animal's health is being seriously affected, surgical operations can be performed to prevent the horse sucking in air. These are also not entirely satisfactory and they are usually only performed as a last resort.

These two vices often cause indigestion and colic, and crib biting results in rapid and excessive wearing down of the teeth with resultant loss of condition.

The primary cause will usually prove to be idleness and boredom or it may be imitation of another horse. The first three steps, then, are obvious:

(1) Give regular work or keep the horse out of the stable in some way as much as possible. When he must stand in for any length of time, let him have a net of hay to pick at and keep him occupied. Do not make the mistake of providing a salt lick under the impression this will serve the same purpose; it may in some instances, but on the other hand it has been known to encourage the trouble or even to cause it in the first place.

(2) Allow him no opportunity of passing the habit on to others.

(3) Remove all fittings so that there is nothing for him to grasp. Anything that cannot be removed should be smeared with unpleasant tasting anti-cribbing ointment available from saddlers. Muzzling may be necessary except at feeding times.

These measures may be effective for lesser offenders, but for the determined crib biter or windsucker, more is usually required. The object here must be to stop the horse sucking in air or prevent it arching its neck to do so. This is often done with a gullet plate and cribbing strap, which a saddler can supply. Better still, perhaps, is the "flute bit" which is also obtainable from a saddler; this has a perforated hollow mouthpiece and effectively prevents air being sucked in.

Crib biting or windsucking may sometimes be developed from a habit of licking the walls, which again, is quite often due to boredom, and regular work is then the remedy. In other instances, however, the fault lies in the food, which may be inadequate, or with insufficient bulk (fibre) or lack of minerals.

Kicking. The problem of the kicker is one that receives, possibly, too little attention; that such-and-such a horse is a kicker is so often accepted as an unpleasant but unalterable fact, no steps being taken to find out the reason and deal with it accordingly. What is generally the reaction to such a horse? Nine times out of ten it is, "Look out for that one, he kicks!" or "Give him a taste of the 'old one-two'" – reaching for a whip. This attitude does not get one very far. First, endeavour to find the cause; there is a reason for everything and therefore, barring exceptional and some long-standing cases, there is a cure.

It is an accepted fact that mares are more likely to kick than geldings, but this usually shows itself during the oestrus period when, obviously, allowances must be made and due care taken not to aggravate ticklishness. With considerate handling, the tendency to kick at these times will gradually decrease and eventually disappear completely. Bullying is no help in such circumstances.

Another cause of kicking in the stable can be lack of work and boredom.

In rare instances, small red spiders, known as harvest mites, may become trapped in bedding at harvest time. These mites bite the skin around the fetlocks, causing extreme irritation, and affected horses may kick out in response. The small mites can usually be seen and the problem is cured by changing the bedding and treating the legs with an anti-parasitic wash.

It is not unreasonable that kicking may be expected from a youngster with a strenuous objection to being handled, and such an animal must be taught he has nothing to fear. The 'old one-two' could hardly be described as a remedy for him, he needs to be handled regularly and to become accustomed to having what he probably regards as "liberties" taken with him. Should he be very difficult, try stroking his hindquarters with the padded end of a long pole. Carried out daily, this will soon convince him there is no cause for fear.

Vermin scuttling about the stable may be the culprits when there is kicking at night-time, hence the stable cat's uses.

A few horses do not like the dark and show their disapproval by kicking. Introducing a dim night light will immediately put matters right. If the stable has no electricity, it might be worth trying a low-powered car light (connected to a car battery) for a few nights to see if this has the desired effect.

Strange horses in the next box will occasionally cause kicking at first but this can be expected to right itself as soon as they are no longer strangers. Lose no time in bringing this about, as kicking can soon develop into a vice.

Kicking while being groomed is, in most cases, traced to ticklishness, particularly with thin-skinned animals. The only possible course is extra care when dealing with the more sensitive parts. If the trouble is really serious, and nothing else has any effect, one foreleg can be either held up by another person or strapped up. Since the horse can only stand on three legs for a short time, he should be given opportunities of resting now and then. As an added precaution, provide a thick bed during these operations in case the horse should lose balance.

Lastly, mischievousness may be the beginning of kicking which ends as a vice, and a sharp but fair reminder of stable manners is not out of place. When such a lesson is called for, it need be no more than a sharp rap on the leg that is raised to strike but it should be administered as soon as the leg is moved for kicking. Prompt action of this kind has been known to cure horses for all time, of kicking during grooming, at one lesson. The value of the use of the voice should not be overlooked, the tone being suited to the nature of the case.

Whatever the cause, if kicking at partitions or posts shows signs of continuing, it is an excellent idea to pad these parts with coarse matting, which will not only prevent injury but also

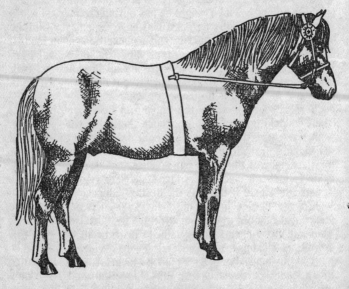

New Forest Pony

deaden the noise; many horses derive great satisfaction from the sound of their own kicking and are encouraged to greater efforts. It will be noticed that in some stables, bunches of gorse or other prickly stuff are used instead of padding so that the horse shall associate pain with kicking and therefore desist. This may effect a cure, or the pain may quite probably cause worse kicking, so if you decide to try this method, watch results carefully.

In connection with kicking at persons, it is worth noting that swishing of the tail is a warning sign, when there are no flies about, and that the nearer one is to the animal when he strikes out, the less is the force of the blow. In grooming the hindlegs it is always wise to make a habit of grasping the hamstring with the free hand, when tension of the leg for a lash-out can be felt in time and the kick prevented by putting the weight on the hamstring and hock.

Rough treatment of a kicker never produces good results, it will be remembered and repaid with interest at the first opportunity.

Weaving. A horse is said to be a weaver when he constantly swings his head, neck and forehand from side to side, almost invariably over the bottom half of the door. In some cases only the head and neck are swung to and fro, producing an effect that reminds one of a spectator at a tennis match, whilst in others the horse actually rocks, often lifting one forefoot after the other or even crossing them.

There is little doubt that weaving is a nervous habit and it is one which is most frequently noticed in wild animals kept in captivity, from which it may be deduced that dislike of being shut in, coupled with boredom and idleness, is the root of the matter.

Less often, a nervous horse will show signs of weaving when moved to a new home or to a different premises – the problem ceasing once it has settled in. From a horsekeeper's point of view, the main objection to the habit is that the constant movement of the head and neck is wasted energy. Weaving is an unsoundness, and, like crib biters and windsuckers, at many horse auctions, horses found to be suffering from these vices, and not so declared, are returnable. Wherever possible, it is best to avoid buying a horse with any of these three vices.

Once formed, the habit of weaving is not easy to break and the owner of several horses may have to guard against imitation by the other occupants of the stable. Attempts are usually made to check the trouble by preventing lateral movement of the head by means of a "weaving" grille attached to the stable door. This has a "V"-shaped hole for the horse to put its head through, but prevents it from moving sideways. If the horse weaves inside the box, it may be tied up to short pillar reins, but this is merely treating the symptoms and not the cause.

The first thing to do is to ensure that the animal has sufficient regular work or exercise and that he does not spend unnecessarily long periods idle in the stable. To this end, as much use as possible must be made of any available grazing in suitable weather; it will frequently be found that such a horse is a "bad-doer" in the stable but picks up wonderfully and is far more "alive" at his work when kept in the open. At such times as he has to be stabled, let there be something to occupy his attention, a hay-net or even a salt lick – in the case of a weaver a salt lick seldom leads to the other vices of crib biting or gnawing at the walls. Imitation of weaving by others is not such a danger as many think and it is debatable whether it is wise to keep a weaver away from his companions, as in doing so one is liable to aggravate the trouble. However, watch other animals carefully and at the first sign of their picking up the habit, remove the first offender.

It would be unwise to guarantee a permanent cure, it having been found that weavers which have spent years at grass immediately resume the old habit when they are back in the stable possibly for the reason given before. However, many good horses are confirmed weavers and show no sign of the loss of condition usually foretold for their kind.

Box-walking. Some nervous horses continually walk their boxes in a similar manner to caged zoo animals. Such horses tend to be "poor doers" because they use up too much energy by being continually on the move and they also do not rest sufficiently. Another annoying habit of nervous horses is failure to eat up properly – such animals are sometimes known as "shy feeders". These horses are also often very difficult to deal with. If given much exercise, they become very thin as their lack of appetite does not keep them in good enough condition to withstand the work. Animals with both these problems often benefit from a companion. If a suitable horse, pony or donkey is not available to share the stable, various other animals, including goats, sheep, chickens, rabbits and cats, have all fulfilled this role successfully. Some competition for the manger has brought many a reluctant feeder to its senses!

11

COMPOSITION OF FOODS
AND SUITABLE RATIONS

In his natural state, the horse satisfied all his food requirements from grass, but he was able to change his pasture at will to find the best food, and seldom travelled at more than a walking pace, grazing as he went, except in escaping from enemies. Under domestication, his size has increased and he is required to work, therefore needing a more concentrated diet, in a balanced form, to maintain a larger body and supply additional energy.

To understand the requirements of a balanced ration it is necessary first to know something about the constituents of food, which, for animal feeding, may be grouped into five recognised classifications. It is not enough, however, to supply concentrated nourishment alone; owing to the nature of his digestive apparatus, bulk (fibre) is essential. The constituents and their uses are:

Proteins. These are flesh-formers, nitrogenous compounds which are split up and simplified by the processes of digestion into a form which the bloodstream is capable of absorbing. Their purpose is mainly to make good the normal wear of tissues and provide for growth. A deficiency will be met by the system robbing the muscles of protein, while too much will lead to ill effects on the digestion and skin, diarrhoea from irritation in the intestines, and strain on the kidneys. A slight excess, however, can be stored by the body as a reserve of energy.

Cereals, particularly oats, are the traditional means of supplying protein to horses. However, the protein content of oats can vary considerably (between 6 and 13%), and manufactured cubes or nuts are now extremely popular as horse feeds because their protein content can be strictly controlled, making it easy to give the right protein content for an individual horse's requirements. Thus a "creep feed" for a growing foal, which has the highest demand for body-building proteins, may contain 16% protein, and feed for a lactating mare, 15%; whereas concentrate feed for a racehorse, or animal undertaking similar exercise, would contain 14% protein. In comparison, horse and pony nuts fed to adult animals doing light work need only contain around 10.5% protein.

Although extra protein is required for working horses, it can sometimes make them "hot up" and difficult to handle. If too much protein is fed, digestive, circulatory and muscle problems can arise. The protein intake must be carefully regulated (on a daily basis) according to work and the horse's condition. If, because of lameness, bad weather or any other reason, a horse cannot be exercised, its protein ration must be cut back accordingly or problems are very likely to occur.

Fats and Carbohydrates. For nutritive purposes these are comparable with each other and have similar functions, producing heat to maintain the body temperature, energy for work, and adding to the reserve store of fat and energy. They are present in all green foods and grain; linseed is particularly rich in fats, with a percentage of 35–40 in the whole seeds, and about 10 in the cake. Carbohydrates exist in oats (which are also rich in digestible oil), barley and maize at 57–70%.

Minerals. Small amounts of various minerals are required on a regular basis in a horse's diet to keep it healthy. At grass, these are normally provided in sufficient quantity in the herbage, but in the stable they must be added to the ration in some form or other. Manufacturered concentrate feeds normally contain minerals and trace elements in amounts sufficient for a horse's needs, but if the horsekeeper is mixing his or her own feed, it will be necessary to add a mineral supplement to the ration. The minerals which are required in the largest amounts are those needed in bone formation – especially Calcium. This is why Calcium-rich limestone soils are favoured as horse breeding areas. A limestone supplement is helpful for growing horses and stabled animals on some diets. Certain feeds, particularly bran, maize, and oats contain little Calcium and high levels of Phosphorus. Too much Phosphorus can suppress Calcium uptake, so that it may be necessary to add a Calcium supplement (limestone) to the ration to keep the Calcium/Phosphorus ratio in the diet in the correct proportions (1.5:1).

Herbivorous diets are generally low in salt and all horses will benefit from additional salt. Although table salt is satisfactory (30 gms, 1 oz daily), using mineralised salt, in which other minerals have been added, ensures that the horse receives a supply of other trace elements as well. The choice between salt licks, lumps of rock-salt in the manger, or mineralised salt sprinkled on the food, is a matter of personal preference.

Hunter

Profuse sweating results in the loss of large amounts of fluid, and minerals and electrolytes. A mineral and electrolyte supplement is to be recommended for all horses regularly performing strenuous exercise. During long-distance endurance rides, horses can suffer very large losses in minerals and electrolytes. If these are not replaced there can be serious consequences, including collapse and death. Anyone taking part in this type of riding should seek veterinary advice about giving minerals and electrolyte supplements before and during the ride.

Fibre. Although supplying some energy and fat, the chief use of fibre is to provide bulk and assist in the digestion of concentrated foods. Its value in horse feeding also lies in the distension of the stomach and capacious intestines, giving that necessary "comfortable" feeling. Bad habits and stable vices are more common when rations composed almost entirely of quickly-eaten concentrates are fed. Chewing fibre would normally occupy most of a horse's day. By reducing the fibre content of the diet unnecessarily, a horse is left with little to do to occupy itself and many behaviour problems begin from the resulting boredom. Hay and straw supply the greatest bulk, being 25–30% fibre but straw has practically negligible food value.

Water. Water is the commonest but most important of all foods; animals can live longer without solid food than without water. Water is required to aid digestion and for many internal body functions. Some feeds, such as grass and vegetables, are composed mainly of water (70–90%), but the bulk of a horse's daily needs must be provided by drinking water. Horses will drink between 36 and 67.5 litres (8–15 gallons) of water daily, and wherever possible they should have access to an ad lib. supply. If water is always available, a horse will naturally regulate its intake according to its needs. Horses are normally "fussy" about water; it must be clean and free from any odour or taint, and soft is preferred to hard, although the latter is often recommended for growing stock on account of the lime content.

In addition to the foregoing, the ration must contain small percentages of the various vitamins. These are obtained naturally when grazing, but when grass is conserved (hay) much of the vitamin content is lost – hence the value of giving fresh vegetables (carrots, apples, etc.) to stabled horses. Brief details of the vitamins needed by horses are given as follows:

Vitamin	*Purpose*	*Source*
'A'	Growth and protection from infection.	Green Foods and Carrots.
'B'	Growth, nervous system and heart.	Green Foods, Roots and Grain.
'C'	Healthy Blood Supply.	Green Foods.
'D'	Healthy Bones and Teeth.	Notably Cod Liver Oil – a valuable addition to the diet of growing stock.

BALANCED RATIONS

A balanced ration is one containing the correct proportions of proteins, fibre, carbohydrates and fats, together with the required amounts of vitamins and minerals. When a manufactured concentrate food is used (nuts or cubes), nearly all the work is done for you because the manufacturers take a lot of trouble to ensure that the proportions of the various nutrients are correct. Working out a horse's requirements is then a matter of deciding how much of the total feed will be fibre and how much will be concentrate. If you are making up your own rations, you will have to "balance" the proportions of the various ingredients yourself so as to provide all the animal's requirements.

Making up a Ration. Feeding horses remains an art, not a science. Although guidelines can be given for the amounts that should be given and the relative nutritive values of different feeds, each horse must be treated as an individual and its feeding assessed daily. The weather, the amount of work being done, the condition of the horse's body and individual variation in the ability to digest and convert food, will all entail adjustments to rations. The success, or failure, of any feeding regime ultimately depends on how the horse looks and behaves. Getting the balance right is sometimes difficult for the novice horseowner, so that "balanced" formulated rations can take away much of the guesswork. Even so, continual minor adjustments will be necessary.

The first factor to consider when making up a ration is the total amount of food required. Here, some idea of the horse's weight is helpful. Weighbands are widely available which measure a horse's girth – giving an approximate weight corresponding to the girth. For those not possessing such equipment, a fairly accurate weight can be calculated as follows:

Weight in kg = girth squared in cm, multiplied by the length from the point of the shoulder to the point of the hip (measured in cm), divided by 8400.

Weight in lbs = girth squared in inches, multiplied by the length from the point of the shoulder to the point of the hip (measured in inches), divided by 241.3.

The total amount of daily feed required by any horse will be between 2 and 3% of its bodyweight. The minimum amount needed for body maintenance is 2% of bodyweight. Mature horses doing no work should remain in good health and condition if this amount is provided.

When turned out in summer, the grass should provide all a horse's maintenance requirements, provided of course, that the grazing is adequate and not over-stocked. In winter, not only is there less grass, but what little grass there is, is of much less nutritional value than growing summer grass, so that it will almost certainly be necessary to give hay to any horse that winters out.

When horses are stabled for all or part of the time, yet doing no work, it may be possible to supply all their maintenance needs by feeding good quality hay only. However, depending on the time of year and the individual animal, it may be necessary to feed a concentrate supplement – making up to 20–30% of the total feed. Part of the art of feeding is deciding whether your horse's maintenance needs can be met by hay alone, or whether concentrates are needed and if so, how much.

Extra feed (above the basic maintenance requirements to keep the horse healthy and in good condition) will be necessary for growing animals, for pregnant and lactating mares and for horses in work. In these situations, not only will more food be required (2.5–3% of bodyweight), but the composition of the ration will alter, in that the additional needs for protein and energy cannot be provided by fodder alone and these must be given in a concentrated form (nuts, cubes, oats and other alternative feeds). The ration of roughage to concentrate will vary between 70:30 for a horse doing light work, up to 40:60 for a horse doing regular heavy exercise. Growth, pregnancy, and lactation require extra protein to provide for the additional demands which they make on the horse's body. More food will be needed for maintenance than a similar-sized animal would require, and a high proportion of the ration must be concentrate (60–70%). Concentrate feeds for breeding animals and young stock will have a higher protein content (15%).

Fig. 5 gives an idea of the feed requirements of different horses, but it must be stressed that this chart should be used ONLY as a guide and must be adapted to suit the needs of the individual animal.

For example, an adult 14.2 h.h. pony weighing 350 kg (just over 750 lbs) and doing no work, would require 7 kg (15 lbs) of feed daily. This could be given entirely as fodder (good quality hay), but the animal might benefit from up to 20% of the ration being given as concentrates (1½ kg or 3 lbs). A fit 16.2 h.h. horse being given two hours strenuous exercise daily (medium to heavy work) and weighing 500 kg (1,100 lbs) would need a total ration of 2½% of its bodyweight, i.e. 12.5 kg or 27½ lbs of feed daily. Because the horse is doing medium to heavy work, the fodder to concentrate ratio must be about 50:50. The ration could, therefore, be divided into 6.5 kg (just over 14 lbs) of hay and 6 kg (13 lbs) of concentrate.

It must always be remembered that all feeding recommendations are only guidelines. Old horses (over 16) invariably require more feed. Thin-skinned animals (in winter) and horses that have been clipped will need extra rations. There is also considerable variation between different breeds and types of

CALCULATING FEED REQUIREMENTS

A rule of thumb when calculating the horse's daily requirements is as follows:

Work category	Definition	Daily feed requirement as a percentage of body weight	Roughage: Concentrate ratio
Maintenance	Maintaining body systems, weight, temperature and muscle tone, and minimum exercise necessary to maintain circulation, respiratory efficiency and general health.	2	70-100:0-30
Light	Maintenance plus daily walking exercise of approximately 30 minutes, or one hour's quiet hack three times a week.	2	60-70:30-40
Light to medium	Maintenance plus daily quiet hacking of approximately one hour's duration, or daily 30 minutes schooling session (50% trot, 50% canter and walk).	2-2.5	60-70:30-40
Medium	Maintenance plus daily hacking, approximately one to two hours duration, including some cantering and jumping, or daily 30-60 minutes schooling (50% trot, 50% canter and walk).	2.5	50-60:40-50
Medium to heavy	Maintenance plus daily active hacking of two hours duration (including some cantering and galloping) or up to three hours of light hacking, or schooling split into two sessions, each of one hour's duration and including cross-country schooling.	2.5	40-50:50-60
Heavy	Maintenance plus daily active hacking of two to three hours duration, plus 40-60 minutes schooling, including some jumping, or hunting two to three times a week. Competitive marathon driving, flat racing, three-day-eventing and long distance training.	2.5	40-60
Strenuous	Maintenance plus competitive long distance riding (more than 30 miles) Steeplechasing. Three-day-eventing.	2.5-3	30-40:60-70
Growth - 1st year to 18 months		2.5-3	30:70
18 months to 3 years		2.5	50-60:40-50
Last 90 days of pregnancy		2.5-3	30-40:60-70

Chart taken from "Feeding Facts" published by D J Murphy Ltd by kind permission of the authors, Deborah Lucas M.Sc. and Elizabeth Launder M.Sc.

Fig. 5 Calculating Feed Requirements

horses in their ability to convert food; some ponies get fat on very little feed, while some Thoroughbreds are almost impossible to keep in good condition no matter how much they are given.

A horse's temperament will also have to be taken into account; phlegmatic animals requiring less feed than "highly strung" individuals, which often need extra feed to keep them in condition. These are just a few of the factors that must be taken into account when making up a ration. They will all require some minor adjustments to the basic guidelines in order to suit the needs of an individual horse.

12

TYPES OF FOODS
AND THEIR USE

Horse feeds can be divided into fodder, concentrates, alternative feeds, and supplements. Fodder provides the bulk of the ration and contains the fibre which is essential for normal equine digestion. If the fodder is of good quality it will provide all of the horse's needs for protein and energy. However, if the horse is doing regular exercise, larger amounts of protein and energy will be needed and the animal may be unable to consume sufficient fodder to provide this. A more concentrated form of food (sometimes referred to as "hard feed") is needed. To add variety to the diet, to keep the horse interested in its food and to avoid the problem that can sometimes arise of the animal becoming too "hot" and unmanageable when given large amounts of concentrate food, other alternative feeds are often substituted for part of the fodder or concentrate ration.

Certain minerals, trace elements, vitamins, amino-acids and electrolytes must also be provided in a horse's diet if it is to remain healthy. These are particularly important during pregnancy, in growing animals and in performance horses. Many compounded rations contain these in the correct amounts, but if horsekeepers are making up their own rations, a suitable supplement will need to be included to provide these essential ingredients.

FODDER

Grass. The natural diet of a horse should provide all its nutritional needs during the summer months. In winter, not only does the amount of grass decrease, but so does its nutritional quality. Additional hay and concentrate food will be required for all horses living out during winter, with the possible exception of the hardiest native ponies. Although good grazing will provide sufficient energy for a horse's maintenance and for light work, grass is a very bulky food and a digestive system full of grass is not conducive to exercise. Thus, although horses can be ridden from grass, if they are exercised regularly it is preferable to restrict their grazing for part of the day, and to substitute a small amount of concentrate so as to lessen the bulk of the food.

The nutritional quality of grazing can vary considerably. In general, horses do best on well-maintained permanent pasture where the deep-rooted grasses and plants provide the minerals and trace elements they need. Newly-sown grass or grazing that has had heavy applications of nitrogenous fertilisers, is not recommended for horses; especially not ponies, which are very likely to suffer from laminitis on such grazing.

Hay. This provides all the fibre and bulk needed as a substitute for grass. When of good quality, it can provide all a horse's basic nutritional needs and even allow it to perform some slow light work. The quality of hay varies considerably; well made and well kept, it has a valuable feeding content, but otherwise can be useless or even injurious. Of the types, – clover, meadow and seed (or "mixture", as from a ley), – choice is a matter of individual preference as there is little difference in their nutritional value. Certain grasses, such as Timothy grass, are more nutritious, and hay made from permanent pasture is likely to contain deeper rooted grasses which have a higher mineral content than the shallower rooted plants of new leys.

Old hay is safer to use than new, since the latter is still "making" or undergoing chemical change, which can cause digestive upsets (colic). However, ill-effects are rare, and as long as the possibility is realised and watched for, new hay may be safely fed if circumstances dictate. In the forage trade, hay may be regarded as "old" after Michaelmas day (29 September), but more often "old" hay refers to the previous year's cut (6–18 months old).

To recognise good hay, note its appearance, smell ("nose"), taste and feel. Never yellow, meadow hay cut at the right time and well saved, is greenish when new, but fades slowly with age.

Seed hay is lighter in colour, and clover darker. Dark brown or black patches indicate dampness and mould. Meadow hay, and sometimes seed hay, has a distinctive "nose" known to all – particularly strong when much Sweet Vernal grass is present – but the aroma decreases with age. Badly made hay, which is too wet at harvest, produces many moulds which can seriously affect a horse's health. This hay has a characteristic "fusty" smell which is quite unpleasant when the hay is shaken up. Mouldy hay should **NEVER** be fed to horses.

The taste should be slightly sweet, never bitter. In feel, meadow hay is soft; seed and clover, harsher and more brittle. There should be a minimum of weeds. Ragwort and Horse-tails (Equisetum), both common pasture weeds, are poisonous to horses, and hay containing these weeds should not be fed to them.

Hay is normally sold in bales – there being about 50 bales to the ton. As a guide, one ton will occupy about 10 cubic metres or yards. However, the size of bales can vary, as can the weight

The Arab

of hay, depending on dampness and how much it was compressed at baling.

Although good quality hay is a valuable feed for horses, there is increasing evidence that the mould spores from hay can be a major source of ill-health. An allergy to these spores causes lung problems and a chronic cough – a condition known as Chronic Obstructive Pulmonary Disease (COPD). Even the best quality hay produces some mould spores and may give rise to symptoms in sensitive horses, particularly if the stable ventilation is inadequate.

Poor quality ("fusty") hay is a serious health risk for any horse, and should not be fed under any circumstances. By soaking hay in water (five minutes should suffice), in a hay-net, the problem of mould spores can be lessened; but for many horses that are allergic to these spores, the best solution is to use alternative forms of fodder which do not produce them. Current farming practices, in which grass is conserved as silage or in big bales, mean that small bales suitable for horses are sometimes difficult to obtain. In these circumstances, it may also be necessary to consider alternative types of fodder.

Lucerne Hay. Lucerne hay has a higher feed value (protein content) than ordinary hay. It is not widely available in the U.K., but is a good feed for horses. Dried Lucerne products are available and make good alternative forms of fodder.

Chaff. This is finely chopped hay or oat straw. It can be cut at the stable, using a chaff-cutter, or bought ready-made. It is often mixed with the rations of horses in work which are eating large amounts of concentrates. It provides fibre in the ration and also slows down the speed at which the horse can eat, thereby avoiding digestive problems which arise if the animal "bolts" its concentrates.

Dried Grass. As a meal or nuts, which must be soaked overnight before feeding, this form of conserved grass is much under-used as a horse feed. It is highly nutritious, and horses and ponies doing light work can do very well when fed on it. It is particularly suited for horses that are allergic to mould spores in hay.

Silage. Silage is a perfectly acceptable way of conserving grass to feed horses. Individually-packed silage products specifically designed for equine use are available, which are ideal for horses that suffer from COPD. Contamination of silage can be a problem, and any bags that have been punctured should be discarded and not used. For the same reason, big bale silage should NEVER be fed to horses. This form of silage is particularly prone to contamination with soil bacteria, and fatal cases of botulism have occurred when horses have been fed on "big bales". Clamp silage does not appear to pose the same risk, and has been fed safely to horses as an alternative fodder.

CONCENTRATES

Oats. This type of grain has been found to be easily digested and to have the best energy value for horses, and has been used as "hard feed" for them for centuries. Good quality oats should have the minimum of husk and should be plump, short, hard and dry. Oats of at least a year old are preferable as they need to mature and dry out. The slight chemical changes taking place in new oats give rise to fermentation and possibly to digestive troubles. Oats can be fed whole, or steamed by adding boiling water (boiling the grains themselves destroys vitamins). Whole grains may pass through the horse's system undigested, so to overcome this problem oats are usually rolled or crushed. However, once treated in this way, they must not be stored for any length of time. If not used within three weeks, their nutritional value declines.

Oats are rich in energy, and must be fed strictly according to work. The reason why they cause some animals to "hot up" is not understood, but great care must be taken in feeding them to some horses and ponies if they are to remain manageable. Over-feeding of oats above requirements can lead to digestive and other problems. If a horse cannot be exercised for any reason, its hard feed must be cut back immediately. Problems such as azoturia and lymphangitis can arise if this is not done.

Compound Feeds – Nuts and Cubes. Compound feeds, containing a carefully blended mixture of ingredients, have many advantages and can take much of the guesswork out of horse feeding. In the traditional system where the feeder makes up his or her own rations from oats and other ingredients (sometimes referred to as "straights"), the quality of every batch of each ingredient must be assessed, and the ration adjusted accordingly. The manufacturers of compound feeds can buy in bulk, selecting the best-quality ingredients at a competitive price. They also analyse and test their products to ensure that the nutritional quality does not vary; which avoids a problem that can arise when home-mixed rations are used. There is no way of telling what ingredients are contained in compound feeds, and some locally-made products may contain feeds of inferior quality compared to those of larger commercial manufacturers. It is therefore essential to buy products made by a reputable manufacturer.

During the production of cubes, the various ingredients are mixed and milled to a fine powder before steam or molasses are added to help bind the material when it is compressed into a pelleted form. Horses on home-mixed rations can differentiate and reject less palatable ingredients, which they are unable to do with compound feeds. However, care must be taken that animals do not "bolt" cubes without chewing them first, otherwise "Choke" and other digestive problems can occur. During the mixing process, minerals and trace elements and vitamins are added in the correct proportions so that there should be no need to feed a supplement. It is important always to follow the manufacturers' instructions when feeding compound feeds and to feed according to the horse's weight. Horses and ponies fed on nuts and cubes will drink correspondingly more water than those fed on "straights", and allowances should be made for this.

Specific compound feeds are produced which are tailor-made for horses at different stages in life or doing different kinds of work. These are variously described in terms such as "Horse and Pony Nuts", "Racehorse Cubes", "Stud Cubes", "Coarse Mixes" and so on. They can be divided into five basic types, according to their protein and fibre content, as follows:

● A low protein (10%), relatively high fibre (15%) nut suitable for feeding with hay, for horses and ponies in light work.

- A high protein (14%), low fibre (9%) nut for horses in hard work.
- A high protein (15%), low fibre (5%) compound for young, growing horses, and mares during the last third of pregnancy.
- A low protein (10%), high fibre (40%) "coarse mixture" designed to supply the complete nutritional needs of horses and ponies in light work, with little or no hay being fed. (If work is increased, it will be necessary to add a low fibre/high protein concentrate to this ration.)
- A grain balancer, designed to add to the traditional diet of hay and oats to balance the ration.

It should be stressed that all these feeds have been formulated to provide a balanced ration for the horse. Adding extra ingredients when feeding nuts or cubes at the recommended rate is not only unnecessary, but can "unbalance" the nutritional content of the diet, which could be detrimental to the animal's health.

ALTERNATIVE FEEDS

Barley. This is sometimes used as a substitute for oats. It is of similar nutritional value but not so well digested. It has the advantage that it is less likely to cause a horse to "hot up". Whole barley grains are not well-digested, so that this cereal is usually crushed, rolled or flaked for use as horse feed. Most often it is boiled (by bringing to the boil and simmering for 4–6 hours to split the grains) for feeding to horses. Boiled barley is an ideal "pick-me-up" after a hard day's work. It can also be useful to help put condition on a thin horse, to tempt a shy feeder to eat, or to provide variety in the diet of a horse in work.

Bran. The husks of wheat have been traditionally fed to horses with oats. Dry bran causes constipation, whereas wet bran has a mild laxative effect. For this reason, bran mashes – made by adding boiling water to dry bran, thoroughly mixing it and allowing it to cool to body heat before feeding – have been traditionally given to stabled horses in work (once or twice a week) to try and prevent impaction (constipation). Bran mashes are also sometimes used to disguise medicines or to encourage invalid horses to eat. Bran has very little nutritional value, and is used mainly to provide bulk to the diet. It has a high phosphorus content and must be fed sparingly, or bone problems, due to interference with calcium levels in the body, can occur.

Maize. This type of grain has a high carbohydrate (energy) level but a relatively low protein content, so that an additional source of protein is usually required to "balance" the ration when maize is fed. The whole grains are indigestible unless boiled or soaked for several hours. For this reason, flaked maize is usually fed. Maize tends to be fattening and can be useful to put condition on a thin horse. It is not recommended for horses in heavy work, but 1 kg (2 lbs) can be given with oats and chaff, together with beans or some other form of protein, as a ration for horses doing moderate amounts of work.

Wheat. This is relatively indigestible and not a suitable feed for horses.

Linseed. The seeds of the flax plant have a high protein and oil content, but are low in some amino-acids. Linseed is useful for putting on weight and improving the quality of a horse's coat. It must ALWAYS be boiled before feeding as the fresh seeds contain a substance which is potentially poisonous to horses. It is normally fed as a mash or gruel, especially in winter. A twice-weekly feed of 113–226 gm (¼–½ lb) of the seeds, weighed before cooking, is given – horses being unable to absorb more than this amount. The linseed is soaked for 24 hours before being brought to the boil, and allowed to cool before feeding.

Sugar Beet. This is a popular alternative feed because it is a good source of energy and fibre which can usefully be included in the ration of a horse not doing fast work, and does not cause a horse to "hot up". If fed in excess, it can have too laxative an effect. It is available as dried pulp or cubes which must be soaked for 12 hours before feeding. Insufficient soaking of sugar beet is a frequent cause of both "Choke" and Colic (pain arising when the beet swells in the horse's stomach after coming into contact with gastric juices). Great care must be taken to ensure that sugar beet is soaked properly, and also to ensure that no horse can break into the store room and eat the dry material.

Field Beans. These are high in protein and may be included in small amounts in rations, to provide a source of protein (e.g. to balance maize). They do, however, tend to make horses "hot up" and must be fed sparingly.

Molasses. This is high in energy and is available as a liquid or meal form. Since horses have a very sweet tooth, molasses is a useful food to tempt "shy feeders" or sick horses to eat; one or two tablespoons of the liquid being added per feed. It is also a useful way of disguising medicines in food.

Succulent Foods. To keep a stabled horse interested in its food, it is always beneficial to give it some fresh green feed. This also helps to supply some vitamins, has a mild laxative effect and helps to satisfy a horse's natural desire for something to chew. Carrots and other root vegetables such as swedes, mangles, turnips, beetroots and parsnips can be fed, after washing and cutting up into slices. Square or round pieces must not be fed as they may cause "Choke". Apples are always especially appreciated. Half-a-kilo (1 lb) is sufficient to begin with but this can be gradually increased to 1 kg (2 lbs).

ADDITIVES AND SUPPLEMENTS

Many different types of mineral, trace element, amino-acid, vitamin and electrolyte supplements are produced for horses. If home-mixed rations are used, it will certainly be necessary to include a mineral, trace element and vitamin supplement. If compounded feeds are fed correctly, additional supplements should not be necessary. Supplements are often given to performance horses in order to keep them in peak condition. While horses which are fed large amounts of oats (which are low in lysine) may benefit from a supplement containing this amino-acid, and horses that have had muscular problems can derive benefits from Vitamin E and selenium supplements, the need for additional supplements in fit, healthy, correctly-fed horses is questionable – with the exception of endurance horses.

Supplements may be deemed necessary to improve skin or hoof quality or to correct bone troubles. When such problems arise, it is always advisable to seek veterinary advice whether supplements are necessary and, if so, which is the most appropriate. Pregnant and growing animals have an extra demand for minerals and trace elements which must be incorporated into their diet. Bone trouble due to lack of calcium is the problem most often encountered, and it is advisable to include a limestone supplement in the ration of brood-mares and growing stock. A limestone supplement can also be necessary for working horses to correct a calcium/phosphorus imbalance, which may arise when large amounts of oats are fed with bran or maize – all of these are high in phosphorus and can upset this balance. Bone meal contains equal amounts of calcium and phosphorus and should not be used as a source of calcium as it will not correct calcium/phosphorus imbalance.

Salt. An adequate salt intake is essential to keep horses healthy. Since the salt content of fodder is often insufficient to provide this, some form of salt supplement is always advisable. The best method is to give the horse control over its own intake by providing a salt lick or rock salt in the manger. Alternatively, between 30 and 120 gms (1–4 oz) of salt can be mixed into the rations each day.

13

PRACTICAL FEEDING

There is no rule of thumb method in feeding; the most carefully compiled chart can be no more than a rough guide, and one is not expected to follow it slavishly. Circumstances must be taken into account, age, constitution and temperament, work, the time of year, weather conditions, and, not least, unaccountable factors in the make-up of the horse which can only be allowed for from experience with the individual animal. These points, particularly the last, apply equally well to most aspects of horse keeping. It has been truly said that only one man can feed a horse – the one who spends most time with it and understands, more or less, its character and peculiarities. Correct feeding calls for knowledge, experience, observation and intelligent use of observation, but there are certain principles that may be laid down.

When measuring the quantity of food to be given, it must always be done by weight, not by volume. Variations between different batches of the same feed (particularly cereal grains) can mean that too much or too little is being given if the weight of a scoop is not checked. Another point worth stressing is that balanced foods are balanced – diluting them by adding other feeds, with the well-intentioned aim of providing variety, can upset the balance between the various components of the diets (particularly minerals) with possible harmful effects.

Food Quality. Buy only the best. Money saved by buying poorer quality food is usually insufficient to balance its inferior feeding value. Trying to penny-pinch may result in your horse losing condition and may even compromise its health. Poor quality hay should be avoided at all costs – fusty hay should not be fed to horses under any circumstances.

The Clydesdale

Feeding Times. Horses are creatures of habit and appreciate regular meals, so try to feed your horse at the same time each day. For its size, a horse has a very small stomach – its capacity of 8–15 litres being about a quarter of that of a similar-sized cow. Thus small feeds should be given at frequent intervals, rather than large feeds at any one time. Ideally, three feeds a day should be given. However, if the horse is doing very little work and fodder is forming the main part of its ration, it is perfectly adequate to feed it twice a day. If it is doing a reasonable amount of work, the quantity of concentrate necessary should be divided into three daily feeds. If very large amounts of concentrate food are necessary because the horse is doing regular strenuous exercise, it may well be necessary to give an additional fourth feed in the evening to avoid overloading the stomach by giving excessive amounts at any one time (see "Daily Routine", page 34).

Horses should not be fed immediately before exercise as a

full stomach will press against the lungs, thereby restricting their function. Nor should they be expected to work for at least an hour after a full feed. If exceptional circumstances make it impossible to allow this time for digestion, the exercise must be restricted to a walk. Similarly, a large feed should not be given immediately on returning to the stable if the horse is tired – its digestive system is not then in a condition to deal efficiently with a large intake.

Changes in Diet. Any changes in diet should be made gradually, to allow the horse's digestive system to adapt. This is important when bringing a horse in from grass, or stepping up its concentrate ration for hard work. Equine digestion is brought about mainly by bacterial fermentation in the large intestine. When the horse is being fed a certain food, the bacteria most suited to digesting it will thrive and will be present in large numbers. Bacteria more suited to digesting other foods will be present in smaller numbers. If the diet is suddenly changed, there will be some bacteria capable of breaking down this new food but not enough to do so properly, which can lead to digestive disorders. There will also be large numbers of bacteria present which were suited to the previous diet. When suddenly deprived of this food, many of these will die and the toxins released in this process may cause colic or even laminitis. Introducing new foods gradually allows the changes in the type of bacteria in the gut to happen slowly without causing digestive upsets.

When a horse is first brought in from grass it should be fed only hay for a few days before starting to introduce a concentrate ration. Likewise, the concentrate ration should be increased slowly in relation to increasing work. If exercise has to be missed because of bad weather or lameness, the concentrate ration can be cut back without the horse suffering ill-effects; but it must once again be built up gradually to its former level when work is resumed.

Food Storage. Horses can be fussy feeders, and wherever possible food should be fresh. Stale, mouldy or dusty food should never be fed. Some feeds do not store well, losing their nutritional value or becoming stale if kept too long. This may lead to wastage when only small amounts are being fed. Here, cubes and nuts have distinct advantages as they can be bought in small amounts in sealed bags, which avoid deterioration and make them easy to store. As has been previously mentioned, plastic dustbins make ideal stores for opened bags of nuts and cubes. All horse feeds should be stored in dry, temperate, vermin-free containers.

Watering. Whenever possible, horses should always have clean fresh water. If this is consistently provided, there should be no need to restrict the horse's access to water at any time, since the animal will regulate its own intake satisfactorily. It is only when a horse has restricted access to water that problems can arise. In this situation, the advice "water before feeding and after exercise" become relevant. Water causes food in the stomach to swell. This can cause colic if large amounts of water are consumed on top of dry food. If a horse does not have a continuous water supply, the water bucket may be removed for an hour after feeding to prevent this trouble.

A stomach full of water will press on the diaphragm and lungs preventing them from functioning properly at exercise. For this reason, horses that have restricted access to water should not be allowed to drink large amounts immediately before work. Contrary to popular belief, no harm results from a hot, tired horse drinking cold water. To be on the safe side, it is best not to allow the animal to drink large amounts while still hot, but rather to let it drink enough to quench its thirst, then, once it has cooled down, give it unrestricted access to water once again.

It has been customary to take the chill off water (by warming it) before giving it to horses, particularly after exercise. There is no evidence to show that cold water is ever harmful to horses, and by giving tepid water one may even be doing the animal a disservice by depriving it of an effective means of cooling down. Ask yourself whether you would sooner have a cool or a lukewarm drink after doing some hard exercise – there is little doubt about the answer you would give.

Although automatic "drinkers" are very convenient, watering by re-filling buckets does allow an assessment of a horse's daily water intake. This can be as little as 18–23 litres

(4–5 gallons) daily, or up to 68–92 litres (15–20 gallons) for a large horse doing strenuous work in hot weather. In some cases, horses which sweat profusely can become dehydrated because of excessive fluid loss and insufficient water intake. Also, insufficient water intake, combined with dry food and too little exercise, are contributing factors to impaction (constipation) – a common problem in stabled horses. (See page 213.)

FEEDING UTENSILS

Hay. This can be fed from a wall-mounted hay rack, from the ground or in a hay-net. The former can be unsatisfactory if mounted high on the wall, as hay seeds may fall into the animal's eyes and dust and mould spores, loosened during feeding, will be inhaled into the horse's nostrils directly below. Although this is the most natural position for a horse to eat, feeding hay on the ground is very wasteful, often being soiled and wasted. A hay-net is the best way to feed hay. Not only does it avoid practically all wastage, but it also makes the horse eat slowly. By giving it time to chew and grind the hay properly before it is swallowed, the food is in a much better state for the intestinal bacteria to work on. It also helps to keep the horse occupied for much of the day, thereby avoiding boredom. Using a hay-net also makes it much easier to weigh the correct amount of hay for each horse – with the help of a simple spring scale kept in the hay-store.

The hay should be shaken up and teased out of its compressed form before filling the net. Any sticks or other foreign material, such as pieces of wire, which may have been inadvertently picked up during baling, can be removed at this stage. A full net will hold 4.5–5.5 kg (10–12 lbs) of hay. When full, the net can be soaked in water for five minutes and allowed to drain before being hung up for the horse to eat. By dampening the hay in this way, the release of mould spores into the stable atmosphere is greatly reduced. This can be a wise precaution for all horses, but it is essential for those that are allergic to these spores (see COPD, page 207).

When hanging a hay-net up for feeding, it should hang at a height just below the horse's normal head position, not higher, where seeds and small pieces of hay may fall into the horse's eyes. The hay-net must be tied so that it remains at its original height. If it sinks to the ground when it is empty, the horse may catch its foot in it.

A
Drawstring passed through ring and down net under strings and pulled out and up tight.

B
Form knot and pull tight.

C
End can be passed through loop for security.
To untie – pull free end after removing from loop.

Fig. 6　Tying a Haynet

This can be prevented by passing the drawstring through the tie-ring and taking it half-way down the hay-net where it is passed under the strings and pulled up tight. A quick-release knot is formed and tightened. With this method, however hard the horse may pull at the net, the only effect is to make the knot more secure. To untie it, it is only necessary to jerk the loose end of the drawstring. For additional security, the end of the drawstring may be passed through the loop of the knot. See illustration above.

Concentrate Foods. These can be fed from fixed, wall-mounted mangers or from removable bowls placed on the ground. Some fixed mangers have tie-rings attached. As with all tie-rings, it is essential to tie a piece of breakable cord to the tie-ring and to attach the halter or head collar rope to this, rather than tying directly to the ring. Some serious injuries have been caused by mangers attached to tie-ropes, which have been pulled from the wall when the horse is startled.

Feeding on the ground is the natural eating position for horses. This encourages discharges to drain down the nostrils.

The fewer fixtures there are in a stable, the easier it is to clean it thoroughly and disinfect it. Removable feeders are much easier to keep clean. It is important to keep mangers clean and to remove all uneaten food. Horses have very keen senses of taste and smell and will frequently reject new food which is mixed with old. When horses are sick and off their food, it is particularly important to remove uneaten food and to give small amounts of fresh food to tempt them to eat. Likewise, it is important to clean water buckets and automatic "drinkers" regularly. The latter are often neglected, particularly in paddocks, when the growth of algae in the water can taint it.

FEEDING PONIES

From reference to the chapter on breeds, it will be seen that our native ponies are hardy little animals thriving on indifferent pasture under severe conditions. In domestication they retain this quality, unless softened by unnatural management, and can live happily at grass all the year round, with some protection against the worst weather. They do, of course, require feeding in winter and should have their ration of hay to replace the grass. Generally speaking, oats should not be fed, but a small amount ($\frac{1}{2}$–1 kg; 1–2 lbs) may be allowed after a hard day's work, such as hunting. Living out, they take their own exercise and are not difficult to handle, but when stabled they soon become frisky and cannot be allowed oats, or their small riders will find them too "hot" or even unmanageable.

14

KEEPING HORSES
AT GRASS

It is well known that good grass contains all the nourishment a horse requires to keep it healthy. The extent to which it is kept at grass will depend upon a variety of circumstances.

Horses that do all their work during the summer months, such as Eventers and Polo Ponies, are sometimes turned out in winter for a well-earned rest. From an economic point of view this has little to recommend it, as the only saving will be in bedding and a certain amount of work. Animals living out in winter will have to be particularly well-fed. Much of their food is used up in maintaining body heat, but properly fed, with a natural coat, horses will be found to be comfortably warm. However, thin-skinned horses (such as those with Thorough-bred or Arab in their breeding), are at a distinct disadvantage in this respect, and the extra feed and rugs needed to keep them in good condition makes wintering out uneconomic and often deleterious to their health.

Hunters are often turned out in summer, when their work is done. A spell at grass gives them a good rest after a hard season, and "Dr Green" promotes good hoof growth and a bloom on the coat of animals that have been stabled all winter. However, measures must be taken to protect animals at grass during summer from flies, which can stop them grazing and make their lives a misery. Care must be taken, when turning out a fit horse, not to make too sudden a change in its feeding. Likewise, a horse that has been turned out during the summer months will have a "grass belly" and will need plenty of time to get fit (2 months). Although it is customary to give horses a rest during a part of the year, it is questionable whether it is necessary to let a fit horse get right out of condition, and in many cases a spell of very light work or a change in routine is as good as a long rest.

The Suffolk Punch

For many horsekeepers, the ideal compromise is a half-and-half system – the horse spending part of the day at grass and the rest in its stable. In winter, the horse would obviously be stabled at night and out by day. Horses outside in winter seldom rest at night, keeping continually on the move to keep warm, while resting during the day. Thus by stabling them at night, they can have a rest and can do light work, or exercise themselves, during the day. In summer, on the other hand, it is better to turn the horses out at night, when they can graze without being pestered continually by flies. When brought in for the day, horses benefit by being bedded down for part of the time so that they are encouraged to rest during the heat of the day if they are not working. They will, of course, need feeding while in; three small hay feeds per day are sufficient if they are idle, but some will make one hay-net last most of the day in such circumstances. Turn them out late in the afternoon and

bring them in again the following morning about eight or nine
o'clock – do not worry about their losing a night's sleep; horses
need but little sleep, three or four hours are all they ask. It may
not be generally known that a horse seldom sleeps for more
than half-an-hour at a stretch, then he will get up, chew a few
mouthfuls of grass, and then possibly sleep for another half-
hour.

Hunters can be rested and still kept in working condition
with this system, if given an hour or two's steady exercise
during the cooler parts of the day and allowed a "light work"
ration. Considered economically, this does not appear to be the
cheapest form of summering, but the owner is amply rewarded
by the well-being of his animals.

Children's ponies are generally kept out all the year round,
and this is no hardship provided that they are hardy
individuals, i.e. a native pony or that type of animal, rather
than a thin-skinned Arab or similar breed. Suitable shelter
must be available for them against heat, flies, driving rain and
cold winds, according to the time of year. The child's pony can,
alternatively, be turned out in term-time and brought in only
when the children return for their holidays. Ponies of this class
cannot be considered in the same way as horses; stabling and
feeding produce little demons jumping out of their skins with
high spirits, while the bitterest weather and only poor feeding
find them still game and fit, but manageable and normally safe.

Remember, however, that Nature is not always perfect or
kind; natural conditions are not always necessarily the best,
and I am by no means advocating neglect of ponies. Careful
observation is necessary to see that they have what they need to
keep them in condition without "getting above themselves".

Although horses have been selectively bred by man to grow
larger, to mature earlier, and to cope with rich diets in order to
do so, many pony breeds have changed little since the Ice Age.
Their digestive systems simply cannot cope with a rich diet. All
too often they are over-fed and this frequently causes laminitis.
Moorland ponies evolved to survive on sparse vegetation, not
on rich pastures. Laminitis is the commonest cause of lameness
in ponies, and nine times out of ten this is caused by turning
them out on lush grass in late spring and early summer. In
many cases it is necessary to restrict grazing at this time of year,

and a few individuals must be removed from grazing altogether to prevent attacks of this very painful disease. Allowing ponies to suffer repeated attacks of laminitis, whether through ignorance or neglect, amounts to cruelty.

It is a tragedy that, too often, ponies are bought for young children by parents without knowledge or experience of horses and are left entirely in their care. Some of the unhappy results we have all seen. I would suggest to all parents that they enrol their children with the Pony Club of the local Hunt, where they will receive first-class instruction and guidance in riding and the care of ponies, and that both should become members of the National Pony Society and take an interest in our fine native breeds.

Feeding Value of Grass. The value of grass as a food in a normal year may be reckoned to last from May until October, and this value will depend upon the nature and extent of the grazing as well as upon the number of horses or ponies kept. A careful watch must be maintained upon the animals to see that they are doing well or if they require supplementary feeding, as they probably will at the beginning and end of the season. If in any doubt, the horses themselves will soon settle the question; when they cease to show interest in good hay, one may be sure the grass is sufficient.

Types of Grasses. Horses do not need such rich grazing as fattening cattle, yet any muddy patch of weeds is by no means good enough. No great experience is needed to judge the suitability of grazing. It is said, with much truth, that horses do well where hedges and trees, particularly the oak and ash, flourish.

To many people, grass is just grass and as such is suitable food for horses. This is not so; many types of grasses are dismissed as "weeds", that is, as having no feeding value themselves and obstructing the growth of useful pasture plants and taking valuable nourishment from the soil. The best pasture grasses are those which, besides being readily grazed, last longest and are not easily stifled by weeds.

Some of the most useful grasses are included in the Fescue types, and of these Meadow Fescue is outstanding, producing a first-class level pasturage. Timothy (Meadow Cat's Tail) and Cocksfoot should have their place, the former making good hay, but Cocksfoot quickly becomes coarse and is unsuitable for hay. Meadow Fox Tail, a hardy, productive grass, is good in pasture and meadow. Another plant also useful in hay, for which it is well-known in the South of England, is Yellow Oat Grass, but the larger Tall Oat has a bitter taste disliked by horses.

Small-growing herbage is needed to produce a level sward by forming "bottom" or "sole" to fill in between the larger "top" grasses. For this purpose, the Rough and Smooth-stalked Meadow Grasses are excellent and liked by grazing animals. Crested Dog's Tail, found with Hard and Sheep's Fescue in sheep pasture on the Downs, is a good, nutritious grass but of little hay value, whilst the Rye Grasses, although giving valuable feed both as grazing and hay, are short-lived on anything but heavy land. Other "sole" grasses are found also in the Fescues; in addition to "Hard" and "Sheep's", there are the "Various-leaved", doing well on light, thin land, and Creeping Fescue on light, wet land. The soil contains nitrogen in an elementary state, and leguminous plants, such as the Clovers and Trefoils, are required to collect and turn this nitrogen into its useful form for grazing animals.

These notes on herbage plants are intended only as a guide to an interesting subject worth closer attention from horse-keepers than it usually gets.

Poisonous Plants. As well known, there are some pasture weeds, wild and garden flowers, shrubs and trees which are potentially poisonous to horses, and these are covered in detail on pages 200–201.

Shade and Shelter. An important point when selecting grazing (when selection is possible) is shelter from a hot sun and protection against driving rain and keen winds, which, even in summer, may be expected. Some protection is afforded by trees and hedges, which should be available on any grazing.

Everyone who has seen horses at grass during the summer will have noticed the annoyance caused by flies, and so persistent are these pests at times that during the day horses are allowed little opportunity of grazing, which explains why a run at grass in hot weather, far from acting as the intended rest and pick-me-up, frequently leads to loss of flesh. Unfortunately, it is in the shade of trees and bushes that flies usually swarm most viciously, driving the distracted animals out again into the glare of the sun, where they stand stamping, shaking their heads and swishing their tails in an effort to get rid of their tormentors. No really effective anti-fly lotion has yet been made.

The provision of a field shelter is desirable to provide protection from the elements in winter, and from flies in summer. It need not be an elaborate structure so long as it is firmly erected and unlikely to suffer or cause damage in high winds. All that is needed is an open-fronted shelter, placed in a position to keep out the rays of the sun during the greater part of the day, where there will be peace from flies and, when necessary, protection from the weather, (i.e. from the prevailing wind). A simple field shelter can be easily and cheaply built of feather-edge boarding on stout timbers sunk firmly in the ground, the sunken parts being well tarred; the dimensions should be not less than those of a loose-box for each horse. Ideally, a hard floor is desirable so that horses have somewhere dry to stand in winter, and this also makes it easier to keep clean. Do not be disappointed if you find this shelter seldom used; it is there if needed, and it will be if flies become too troublesome or the wind too keen. It is also a useful place for feeding in the winter, and horses soon appreciate the little extra comfort it gives them.

Fences, Gates, etc. Having satisfied yourself as to the suitability of the paddock, there are still other points calling for attention.

The ground, fences and hedges should be regularly inspected for dangerous objects; it is amazing what peculiar things find resting places in paddocks which adjoin roads or are situated in suburban areas. Broken bottles, large flints, bricks and other possible causes of injury seem to grow overnight, while hedges and fences only too frequently bristle with barbed wire entanglements. Mole hills, rabbit holes and ant hills should be levelled off, as they are a menace to galloping horses.

Fences and gates must be secure and escape-proof. You may have the finest pasture, yet to most animals there is always an irresistible attraction in your neighbour's. As to the kind of fencing, you will need no warning against that invention of the devil (I usually call it something stronger) – barbed wire, but nearly as dangerous are low, sharp-pointed chestnut palings and spiked iron railings. "Posts and Rails" make the best fencing, perhaps, but any type can be used so long as it conforms to certain standards: it must be sufficiently high to discourage jumping out (usually five feet is ample); strong enough to withstand high winds or the pressure of horses rubbing against it; free from gaps through which a nimble and cunning pony could squeeze; and it must, as already mentioned, present no pointed or sharp portions even remotely capable of inflicting injury. Wherever possible, gates should be in the middle of a fence, rather than at a corner. This prevents animals being cornered and bullied when they are released on being turned out. Hardcore and chippings in the gateway will prevent it becoming a mud bath; horses tend to congregate here while waiting for food.

Time and trouble spent on fences and gates in the first place are time and trouble saved later, as probably 50% of the injuries to horses at grass can be traced to neglect in these items. It is worthwhile fencing telegraph poles and electricity pylons and their support cables to prevent horses running into them. Above all, fences and gates must be secure. If a horse gets out on to a road, its owner will be responsible for any damage or injury which it may cause. Likewise, if it enters a neighbour's property, through inadequate fencing, its owner will be liable for any damage it may cause.

If it is possible to adopt a form of fencing which will protect the animal from the attentions and mistaken kindnesses of passers-by, your mind will be relieved of much worry. Many a young horse has been spoilt in temper by tit-bits and unintentional teasing at the fence, and many a horse has suffered or even died from eating unsuitable plants fed to him by well-meaning but ignorant animal-lovers. It is characteristic of most horses that they will accept from the hand that which they would not otherwise eat.

Water. Finally, ensure a constant supply of fresh, clean water. If a natural supply is at hand, in the form of a stream or pond, make certain it is suitable. A stream is obviously to be preferred to any other source, so long as it is unpolluted at any point either in or before reaching the paddock, but stagnant ponds or pools are to be avoided and should be fenced off. For an artificial supply, try to secure a large, easily-cleaned receptacle capable of being quickly filled without undue labour. Failing a proper drinking trough, a time-expired enamelled bath is excellent, being of adequate capacity even for several horses and easily cleaned. The green slime that forms in any water trough is harmless in itself but can harbour injurious germs and parasites and should not be allowed to remain. Do not imagine, because a horse is at grass, from which he certainly obtains some moisture, that water is in any degree less necessary than in the stable. Summer or winter, wet or fine, ample, pure water *must* be available or condition will suffer.

Shetland Pony

MANAGEMENT AT GRASS

Grass is a valuable crop, and as such needs to be carefully tended. Ideally, when horses live out all the year round, there will be a change of grazing available. In this connection two small paddocks are better than a single large one, as one may be rested while the other is in use, and it is worthwhile dividing a large field into two for this reason. Land quickly becomes "horse-sick", the growth of herbage coarse and unpalatable, and before long the pasture is useless as such. When circumstances permit, the resting paddock will be improved by chain-harrowing and rolling towards the end of the winter or in the spring. Harrowing distributes the droppings evenly over the surface, pulls out moss and matted growths of grass and allows air to enter the soil. It is bad practice to leave dung undisturbed, as it destroys for a time the plants beneath, and acts as a reservoir for worm parasites, preventing them being killed off in dry weather. A horse's natural aversion to grazing near droppings is an inbuilt protection mechanism, as there are always more worms in their vicinity. However, this results in ungrazed areas of "rough" containing weeds and droppings and much wasted grazing. Although harrowing will break up and disperse droppings, research has shown that the best means of worm control is to pick up droppings and remove them from the grazing. If this is done twice a week, the worm contamination of the pasture will be kept to a minimum. The horses will also graze the entire area so that there will be no wastage. Worm control is an important part of pasture management. Over-stocking and over-grazing forces horses to eat near droppings, greatly increasing the risk of them picking up worms.

The infective worm larvae can survive the winter on grass, ready to infect horses turned out in spring. However, if the grazing is left horse-free until June, nearly all these over-wintering larvae will have died, and a relatively "clean" pasture will be available for young horses, which are most at risk from worms. Worming horses at grass is essential to keep pasture contamination to a minimum. It is vital that all horses sharing the grazing are wormed, and at the same time; there is little point in only worming one. The most important times to worm are late May or early June, and late August or early September.

Strategic wormings at these times significantly reduce pasture levels of worm larvae. On no account should stable manure be spread on horse paddocks.

Horses will eat the best grass right down and will leave the rest so that patches of long coarse grass result. These must be mowed. Thistles and other weeds must be cut or treated with weed-killer when the paddock is being rested, then removed and burnt. Cattle and sheep graze more evenly and will eat out the areas neglected by the horses. They also have different worm parasites, so that by eating horse worms they effectively clean up the grazing without becoming infected themselves. Rolling helps to level and consolidate the soil, and is necessary when the ground has been churned up by horses' hooves in winter.

It is feasible to take a crop of hay from the resting paddock, and although this is not considered the best practice since, it is said, land kept solely for grazing produces the most suitable grass for this purpose, (the rule applying similarly to land kept for hay alone) yet its advantages may often outweigh its disadvantages. On the other hand, the succulent and nourishing spring grass should not be sacrificed unnecessarily for a small crop of possibly inferior hay. The question of "to hay or not to hay" can only be decided by the horse-owner concerned, having regard to his particular circumstances and according to whether winter hay, whatever its quality, is likely to be more valuable than summer grass.

It may be necessary to apply fertiliser to horse grazing to improve it. Potash and lime may be needed, and soil analysis can be helpful to determine the type and quantity of fertiliser required. However, high levels of nitrogen, which are commonly applied to grassland for farmstock, are not recommended for horse paddocks. There is high risk of laminitis if ponies are turned out on rich grazing which has been treated with nitrogen fertilisers.

The use of top dressing must be regulated according to the nature of the soil, but most grazing land is improved by dressings of lime, kainit, or basic slag.

Feeding. It has already been said that grass normally supplies sufficient fodder from May until October, and that the horse's reactions towards dry feeds can be taken as a guide to his requirements in the way of supplementary feeding. In a good season, horses on reasonable grazing will need only winter feeding if they are left out during the day and doing little or no work. Lack of grass in winter calls for a supply of hay to make good the deficiency in bulk, and a "maintenance ration" of the best hay procurable should be given, preferably divided into two feeds and given in hay-nets. As well, concentrates may be needed to keep up the body temperature, and this should be given in two feeds in the form of crushed oats or nuts or cubes at the "light work" rate, mixed with a couple of handfuls of chaff.

Working. It will be readily appreciated that a grass-fed horse cannot be expected to perform the same amount or type of work as a corn-fed one; fast work should not be asked of him. A working horse should be given a small amount of concentrates on his return, say 1.5 kg (3 lbs) of oats, or equivalent nuts or cubes; when there is a lack of grass he must, of course, receive the appropriate ration according to his size and work.

Being unclipped, there is more likelihood of the animal returning from work hot and sweating, even with the greatest consideration on the part of the rider or driver, and on no account should he be unsaddled or unharnessed and turned loose without first being thoroughly dried and cooled. Failure to observe this elementary precaution may quite easily lead to serious consequences.

The grooming of a horse living out is best kept to the minimum necessary for appearance, since the grease and long hair in the coat are required for warmth and "waterproofing". Dried mud, however, should, from time to time, be brushed from the legs using a dandy brush, to prevent a bacterial dermatitis, known as "mud fever", developing.

General Hints. The process of changing from stable to grass feeding should be gradual to avoid gorging and the harmful effects of a sudden change in diet.

When being turned out into a field for the first few times, it is to be expected that some excitement and impatience will be shown – a few bucks and kicks will be displayed as soon as the horse is free. To safeguard yourself, face him towards the gate while taking off his head-collar, then stand clear. Remember, too, when horses are allowed to pass through a gate by themselves, the gate must be *wide open*, otherwise, in the rush and excitement, serious injuries are possible from knocks and scrapes.

Before horses are finally left at grass for any length of time, unless they are still to be worked regularly, reduce the chances of injuries to each other from kicks by having the hind shoes removed. To prevent splitting of the hoof, if the fore-shoes are also removed, have the lower margin of the wall bevelled or the feet shod in front with grass tips – but in the latter case heed the warning on page 124. Monthly attention by the farrier will still be necessary.

Every day the animals must be examined for any injuries or other troubles. The teeth, also, may need inspection at intervals; the tables of the cheek teeth are not worn to any extent by chewing grass, and the edges may become very sharp.

For the less hardy breeds, and those which grow but little coat in the winter – Thoroughbreds particularly – the "All-Weather" or "New Zealand" waterproof rugs are useful. These rugs, which are made to allow freedom of movement and to right themselves after rolling, are perfectly safe, all being fitted with leg straps or fillet strings to keep them in place. It is very important that they should be of correct size and fitting, and that the leg straps should be properly adjusted so that there is no possibility of either chafing of the legs or of a leg being caught up. Watch regularly, also, for any chafing around the shoulders. The makers will supply full directions regarding the use and fitting of their own rugs. (See also page 64.)

Horses are gregarious animals and appreciate companions, so try to provide yours with one, even if only a donkey. If a donkey is being used for company don't forget to worm it regularly. Donkeys often have lungworms and pass them on to horses (making them cough), even though they themselves seldom show signs.

15

THE FOOT AND SHOEING

If the truth of the old saying, "No foot, no horse", is realised, a good farrier must be considered as one of the best friends of the horsekeeper. An incompetent farrier can, in time, ruin the feet and render a valuable horse useless, but the modern, qualified shoeing-smith is a highly-skilled specialist. He has made a comprehensive study of his art, including not only the actual practice of shoeing, but also its relation with the anatomy of the foot and leg, a subject in which he is well versed. He can rectify many cases of deformity, poor action, etc., and on such matters his advice should always be sought.

At the same time, it is well for the horsekeeper to be conversant with the interesting, elementary principles of the foot and the functions of its various parts.

CONSTRUCTION OF THE FOOT

The foot is constructed of an inner "core" of bones, surrounded by continuous fleshy parts (collectively known as the "Pododerm", or, commonly, the "quick"). These fleshy parts are responsible for their own corresponding horny structures in the protective outer casing, the hoof, the sole, and the frog. The bones within the hoof are the lower portion of the short pastern bone (second phalanx), the entire Pedal or Coffin bone (third phalanx) and the elongated Navicular bone, which lies between the wings of the Pedal bone. The sensitive, or fleshy parts, are considered as they occur in the following sections. These parts are served by numerous blood-vessels, which explains why even a small wound here bleeds profusely. The horny hoof comprises the wall, sole, and frog.

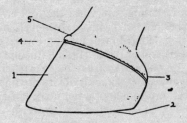

THE HOOF

1. Wall	3. Bulbs of Heels	5. Coronary Cushion
2. Sole	4. Frog Band	

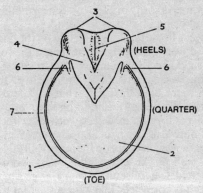

THE HOOF

1. Ground Surface of Wall	3. Bulbs of Heels	6. Bars
2. Sole	4. Frog	7. White Band
	5. Cleft of Frog	

Fig. 7   Parts of the Hoof

The Wall. As its name implies, this is the part of the hard, horny, insensitive casing seen when the foot is flat upon the ground. It can be compared with our own nails and, like them, is always growing. Nourishment for its growth is derived from the Coronary Cushion or Band, a fleshy structure carried at the upper part of the wall and seen as a bulge extending round the Coronet. Toughness and some flexibility are imparted by the presence of a certain amount of water in the horn, evaporation being prevented by a thin layer of hard "varnish", the Periople. The Periople is secreted from the Perioplic Band, a fleshy ring around the top of the hoof, above the Coronary Cushion, noticeable as a white band when the foot is wet.

The parts of the wall are known as the toe, quarters, (that is, the sides) and heels. The toe is the thickest and highest part, the wall gradually becoming thinner and shorter towards the heels, turning inwards here as the "Bars". The "Angle of the heels" formed by the Bars is sometimes known as the "seat of corn" because this area is easily bruised by stones or ill-fitting shoes – such bruising being known as a "corn".

With shoes, a horse takes all its weight on the hoof wall. Even when unshod, very little weight is taken on the sole. The hoof wall is worn down by ground contact in the unshod foot. However, this wear is often uneven – the toes tending to be worn down more than the heels. Thus it is necessary for the farrier to trim the feet of unshod horses to level them. If the horse has a conformation defect, such as a foot that turns inwards or outwards, wear is also uneven. With a foot that turns out, more weight is put on the inner wall of the hoof when the animal walks. The outer wall is less worn so that the conformation defect is actually made worse by the uneven wear, unless it is corrected. Likewise, a toe that turns in wears more on the outer wall, so that the inner wall must be trimmed to level the foot. Inexperienced owners sometimes do not realise that the feet of horses at grass need attention, and, as a result, ponies are all too often encountered with cracked and deformed feet.

In the shod foot there is no wear at the toe, but the constant expansion of the softer horn at the heels wears the heel through contact with the shoe. Trimming ("dressing the foot") is required to correct this. If the shoes are left on more than 4–6 weeks (the time depends on the rate of hoof growth) an overgrown foot results, which, by natural spreading, becomes too large for the shoe and breaks away at the nail holes, or overlaps the shoe with consequent lameness.

"Balancing" the foot. The object of trimming or "dressing" a hoof is to restore its shape, as nearly as possible, to a normal outline. This ensures that the horse's weight is distributed evenly and correctly upon the foot, which is then said to be "balanced".

Foot conformation is important because the shape of the feet affects their flight, and hence the horse's action. Misshapen feet put extra strain on limbs and can therefore be a contributing factor in various types of lameness.

In a normal foot, the front surface of the hoof wall and the pastern (when viewed from the side) should be in a straight line. The heels should also be in parallel to both the pastern and the hoof wall. In the forelimb, this angle is normally between 45 and 50 degrees. In the hind limb, it is slightly more (50–55 degrees). Abnormalities, such as an upright ("boxy") foot, or a long-toe/low-heel conformation, can be altered by repeated corrective trimming, over several months, to restore a normal hoof-pastern axis. Likewise, the sides of the hoof wall must be trimmed to make them level (i.e. an equal distance from Coronet to bearing surface). "Balancing" a foot requires skill, and is an essential part of the farrier's craft.

There is increasing evidence that the additional strain imposed by the all-too-common foot conformation fault of long toes and low heels may be one of the most important contributing factors to the development of both Navicular disease and sprained tendons. This particular fault is one that can easily be corrected by a competent farrier.

The Sole. The outer, horny sole grows from the sensitive or fleshy sole covering the under part of the Pedal bone, and should be concave from the ground surface. Between the wall and the sole is the "white line", a ring of soft horn, the edge of which is visible at the ground surface. The white line allows expansion of the sole when weight is put upon it, and to the farrier indicates the thickness of the wall and the nail-room available.

As a general rule, no paring of the sole is necessary at shoeing, since it flakes away naturally during growth. It used to be the custom to pare the sole until it was "springy" and could be pressed inwards; eventually it was proved that only harm resulted from the practice, which has now ceased as such. However, there are cases where the sole does *not* flake away and must be pared; the skilled farrier recognises the condition and proceeds accordingly. Failure to pare the sole on such occasions may allow the feet to become very long and necessitate extra cutting eventually.

The Frog. If the foot is held up, the frog can be seen as a rubbery, triangular piece of horn projecting below the level of the sole. Growing from the sensitive or fleshy frog, which covers the "Plantar Cushion" situated inside the hoof, it is very elastic and acts as a shock-absorber and non-slip device. It has another function, frequently overlooked, that of assisting in the circulation of the blood supply in the foot when blood-vessels become flattened against the wall by expansion of the structures under pressure. The "Plantar Cushion", extending from the rear-most portion of the foot (the bulbs of the heels) to the Pedal bone, is of very elastic, fibrous tissue resembling the frog in shape, which it assists as a shock-absorber. The comprehensive provision in this region against concussion is necessary because the heels meet the ground before the toe, and the frog and its associated structures must bear the first shock.

The frog, then, to carry out its functions, must always make contact with the ground and should therefore never be pared except for the removal of any "rags". Extra growth is worn away by the friction of contact with the ground and by the forming of ragged portions. Although subjected to so much weight, shock and wear, the frog is rarely injured, owing to its toughness and elasticity, but it may suffer cuts from glass, sharp and jagged stones and picked-up foreign bodies (hence the need to examine feet after work).

SHOEING

Materials. Mild steel is normally used for making shoes,

Thoroughbred

although other materials, notably rubber, have been tried with the object of reducing concussion and providing better grip on slippery surfaces.

As a general rule, the shoe should be no thicker than necessary for the type of work, but should be sufficient to give about four to six weeks' normal wear.

In modern practice, the farrier buys his steel in bars of suitable sections, from which he cuts required lengths to make the shoes, or he may buy machine-made shoes of various sizes. As might be expected, the hand-made article is superior to the machine-made one, and the latter must be finished by hand. The holes are pitched at a sharper angle than is possible with a machine, enabling the farrier to get better position and hold for his nails. The system of welding two old shoes together and working them to make one new one produced a shoe of great toughness, owing to the extra hammering necessary. This system is seldom seen today for typically modern reasons – expensive and poor quality fuel and increased labour costs.

THE SHOE: TERMS AND PARTS

Cover. This refers to the width of the metal and is frequently interchangeable with –

Web. Although "web" may be loosely employed with the same meaning as "cover" (for example, a broad web shoe), it strictly includes also the thickness of the material, that is, the whole cubic area of metal.

Toe and Heel. No explanation of these terms is needed.

Branch. The complete side of the shoe from toe to heel, corresponding to the "quarter" in the foot.

Quarter. The part of the branch between the toe and heel. Thus there are two branches in each shoe.

Bearing or Foot Surface. The surface of the shoe on which the foot rests; the opposite being the ground surface.

Fullering. A fullered shape is grooved in the ground surface, for about half its depth, either all round or for the nail holes only. The intention is to provide increased grip, and, particularly in heavy machine-made shoes, for easier piercing of nail holes. It cannot, as sometimes claimed, make the shoe lighter, since no metal is actually *removed* in fullering. Slipping is prevented, to some extent, not only by the edges of the fullering, but more by the small stones, grit, etc., which collect in the groove.

Calkins and Wedges. A calkin is a projection at the heel of the hind shoe, made by turning a small piece of the metal downwards to give better foothold, and is found especially useful when going downhill on slippery grass. It may be on both, or on the outer heel only, and in the latter case the inside heel must be brought to a similar level by thickening, known as a "wedge heel". It must be remembered that calkins soon wear down and become ineffective. Calkins raise the heel and alter the angle of the foot and are best avoided unless absolutely necessary.

Clips. These are small triangular pieces drawn from the outer edge of the shoe, fitting into shallow "beds" or nicks cut out in the wall of the hoof. Their object is to prevent movement of the shoe backwards or sideways. They should be no larger than necessary for the size of shoe, a short clip with a good base being stronger than a long, thin one, and they may be placed at the toe or at each quarter. On the fore-shoe a toe clip is used. A toe clip can also be used on hind shoes, but most farriers will fit quarter clips because these slightly lessen the risk of over-reaching, that is, striking the heel or back tendon of the forefoot with the toe of the hind. In a horse that brushes (strikes one foot against the opposite fetlock when moving) it is often advisable to have one toe clip and one at the outside quarter to stop the shoe moving to the inside of the foot. In many saddle horses they can be dispensed with altogether – see "Set-up Toe" (page 124) – and often are in racehorses.

TYPES OF SHOES

Plain Shoe. This is a shoe with a flat ground surface, the holes being "plain stamped", that is, without fullering.

Flat Shoe. "Flat" refers to the foot surface of the shoe, which, in this case, covers the bearing surface of the wall, the white line and a small portion of the sole and bars.

Seated Shoe. In a seated shoe, the bearing surface is bevelled or hollowed out at the inner edge so that it makes little or no contact with the sole – the shoe is said to be "seated-out". As has been seen in "Construction of the Foot", page 116, the sole is normally slightly concave and therefore this precaution is only necessary for feet that are flat or have a dropped sole. (The farrier often refers to a flat foot as "fleshy".) There is usually no objection to the sole taking some bearing, which will not cause lameness, and is, in fact, often recommended. Disadvantages of a seated shoe are that it is more likely to be loosened by suction in deep going, and dirt collects in the seating.

Concave Shoe. A concave shoe is ground-seated, that is,

bevelled or hollowed out at the inside edge of the ground surface, making this narrower than the bearing surface. This pattern is commonly used for riding-horses, particularly hunters, for which it is useful as it is less likely to be sucked off in deep, holding ground, and is lighter than an ordinary shoe.

Rodway Shoe. This is a shoe with double fullering, the second groove, on the inner side, not being pierced with nail holes. There does not seem to be much advantage in this pattern except that it may give slightly better foothold, for the same reasons as single fullering. Similarly, it cannot be lighter than a plain shoe. Formerly popular for carriage horses, it is now seldom seen.

Set-up and Rolled Toe. There is little difference between these two, and they may therefore be considered together. At the toe, half the width of the web in the foreshoe is bent up, usually at an angle of about 22 degrees; no clip is used, but the wall of the foot must be rasped back at this part for reception of the turned-up toe. Although sometimes the hind shoe is not set-up or rolled, but has clips at the sides, there is a good case for rolling the toe. This part wears before any other, so that if it is rolled, the whole shoe has a longer life and may therefore be made thinner and lighter, giving increased frog pressure with consequent reduction of concussion and risk of slipping. Since stumbling is frequently the result of putting the toe down first, if the shoe is rolled and shortened at the toe there is less chance of its catching as the heel comes to the ground. For these reasons it seems that many cases of lameness would be avoided by the use of rolled toes, and certainly the ideal requirements are more nearly approached – a light shoe giving sufficient wear for 4–6 weeks and allowing the frog to function.

Grass Tips. These are half-shoes, designed to protect the horn from splitting at the toe. Although intended for horses at grass, they may be useful for ponies doing little work on hard surfaces, or for youngsters on leading exercise. In all instances they must be inspected regularly for looseness, and *removed every four weeks* to rectify uneven growth of the ground surface of the wall. Failure to do so upsets the balance of the foot and imposes strain on the tendons. To fit correctly, the ground surface of the tip and the bare portion of the wall must be level, which necessitates the branches tapering towards the ends. Four nails are required for fixing.

SHOES FOR VARIOUS TYPES OF HORSES

Hunters and Hacks. On account of the similarity of their work, the same pattern of shoe is usually appropriate. For these horses, provision has to be made to counteract the suction of heavy going covered at fast paces, and both fore and hind shoes should therefore have a fullered, concave ground surface. The inner branches must follow the line of the wall exactly, or even be set slightly under to avoid brushing.

The front shoe is usually clipped at the toe, and should be rolled slightly as a precaution against stumbling, but it is suggested again that the advantages of the real set-up toe should not be overlooked. To prevent the heels being trodden on and the shoe pulled off by the hind toe, at the gallop, these should not extend beyond the wall of the foot at the back, and many farriers make them a fraction of an inch shorter than the wall. The heels are also bevelled down to match the angle of the heels of the foot.

There are several ways of treating the hind shoes. Toe clips, although often used, are not recommended. If clips are employed, it is better to place them each side of the toe, which should be "squared off" or even "set back" a little, to avoid over-reaching or "forging" at fast paces in deep ground. ("Forging" is striking the front shoe with the toe of the hind, hence the descriptive terms "clicking" and "clacking", also applied.) Instead of clips, a set-up toe has obvious advantages. The branches need not be shortened, as in the fore-shoe, and, for better grip, the outer heel is sometimes fitted with a small calkin, the inner branch having a wedge heel. Calkins are unnecessary for hacks, as galloping on deep ground can be avoided.

Weights vary from 1.8 to 2.2 kg (4–5 lbs) per set; ponies proportionately according to their size, from just over 1 kg (2½ lbs) for 12 hands in height.

Carriage-type Horses. Since their work is on roads, at slow paces, a heavier shoe can be used, but provision against slipping is necessary, and for this purpose calkins are fitted on the hind shoes. Rodways were commonly employed when carriage horses were numerous. The practice now for this type is usually fullered shoes in front and plain shoes behind, though the hind shoes also are sometimes fullered.

The weight of a set of shoes is about 1.8 to 2.7 kg (4–6 lbs) for lighter animals and up to 3.6 kg (8 lbs) for heavier horses.

Draught Horses. The type of horse to be provided for is one doing slow, often heavy work, which calls for a shoe giving good foothold, particularly when hauling heavy loads. Therefore, large calkins are made on the heels of the hind shoes, which may be wide fitting with the same object, especially as brushing is unlikely at their speeds. To increase foothold, toe pieces may be added – a strip of metal welded on slightly behind the toe. Flat shoes are used, plain when hand-made, but fullered when machine-made, on account of the thickness of the web.

A set will weigh anything up to 9 kg (20 lbs).

Racehorses. For these, two patterns are in use; a light, fullered, concave shoe of mild steel for training, and a fullered, concave "plate", generally of aluminium, for racing.

Training shoes weigh about 680 gms (1½ lbs) a set, whereas racing plates weight 230–450 gms (½–1 lb).

FITTING THE SHOES

Preparing the Foot. As was seen in the description of the construction of the foot, all that is necessary is to remove the growth that has taken place in the wall since the last shoeing. This is done with the "toeing knife" or by using the pincer-like "hoof cutters". The wall is then levelled with the rasp, and beds for the clips cut in the horn either with the same knife or with the curved "drawing knife".

Fitting the Shoe. The first principle of good shoeing is that the shoe must be made to fit the foot. It is not to be expected that at first trial the shoe will be found to be exactly right; it must be worked until it is. But the foot must not be cut and rasped to make a good fit – one would hardly agree to a shoemaker removing a slice of one's big toe to make the foot suitable for his shoe!

The usual method of fitting is by "hot shoeing". The shoe is heated in the fire and then applied to the bearing surface of the wall; by the slight charring of the horn, the farrier judges the fit of the shoe, the size, shape and bearing. If the bearing is level, the hot shoe will mark the horn *evenly* all round, indicating that the foot and shoe meet each other correctly at all points, leaving no "daylight" anywhere. To the uninitiated, hot shoeing with its smoke and smell of burning hoof appears to be a painful process; it is not, of course, nor is the driving of nails through the wall, since the horn is insensitive. On the other hand, the animal can feel even a light touch here, owing to the generous distribution of nerves in the sensitive structures and their close contact with the insensitive parts.

Another method is "cold shoeing" in which the most appropriate ready-made shoe is selected from the stock carried by the farrier. This calls for greater skill and a keener eye, but a competent farrier will produce perfectly satisfactory results using this method.

If there is sufficient wear left in the old shoes, these may be used again, after the excess horn has been pared away, when the process is known as "removes".

Nailing. It will be noticed that the number of nail holes may differ in various sets of shoes. The machine-made ones often have more than the hand-made, but that does not mean they all have to be used; their purpose is to allow the farrier some choice in placing his nails. The least number necessary to keep the shoe in position is the rule, and seven are commonly used, three at the inside quarter, four at the outside. Since the shoe must be securely held throughout its life, the nail-heads are so designed that they do not wear down before the shoe. To achieve this, the "stamp", the tool with which the holes are punched, is wedge-shaped like the nail heads; thus holes and nails make a firm joint throughout the wear of the shoe. A "pritchel" is finally used to open the hole sufficiently at the ground surface for the nail to pass through.

Driving the nails correctly calls for skill, experience and a keen eye. The white band, previously mentioned on page 119, is an indication of the thickness of the wall and therefore of the height at which the points of the nails must emerge. At too sharp an angle they penetrate the wall too low and do not obtain a good hold, being liable to break away the horn at the edge. Driven too high, their shanks come closer to the fleshy lining of the wall than safety permits, and may bruise it (a "nail bind"), or the points may pierce this sensitive structure, causing a "prick". It may be the holes are badly placed in the shoe, either too near the outer edge in the first fault, known as a "fine stamping", or too near the inner edge in the second, known as "coarse stamping". Another reason for these faults is more frequently to be found in the thinness of the wall – some horses have walls "as thin as tissue paper", so that it is a matter of surprise not that they are pricked, but that it happens so rarely. No farrier pricks a foot purposely, and very few do so from negligence, but even with the greatest care, sometimes the point of a nail turns inwards when being driven. Due to the difference in the slope of the wall, nails at the heel are usually driven slightly lower than at the toe.

Clenching. As each nail comes through the wall, its point is immediately twisted off with the claws of the driving hammer to avoid injury if the horse makes a sudden, unexpected movement. When all nails in one shoe have been driven, the farrier places the closed jaws of his pincers against each stub, or broken end, while hammering the head of the nail home. This turns over and forms the "clenches", which he completes by hammering flat into the wall and smoothing over with the rasp. Here it will be noticed that he does not, or should not, rasp above the clenches; to do so would be pointless and harmful, and remove some of the periople unnecessarily.

Clips. When preparing the foot, small shallow beds were cut in the wall in appropriate positions for the reception of clips, which are now hammered in flat against the wall.

Finishing. The final touch is to run a corner of the rasp around the edge of the wall where it meets the shoe to remove any small shreds of horn and bevel the wall slightly to prevent splitting. Note that only one or two quick strokes are required, and only at the *edge* of the wall. Excessive rasping down the lower part indicates that the toe of the shoe is too short and the foot is being "dumped" to fit. Dumping removes some of the protective periople and leads to brittleness of the horn, as did the old practice of sandpapering around and above the nails. Probably it will make a neat-looking finish, especially with a tasteful coating of hoof-oil, but good shoeing needs no beautifying and the neatest effect does not mean the best workmanship.

NON-SLIP SHOEING

In winter, extra precautions against slipping may be necessary, at least for horses working on icy roads, and there is a choice of several methods:-

Roughing. Although the term "roughing" is generally loosely applied to all anti-slipping devices, it strictly refers to a particular modification of the shoes themselves. The shoes are removed, and if calkins are not already present these are formed by turning down the heels. They are then sharpened to a chisel edge, the one at the outer heel lying across the shoe, the other pointing forward. Occasionally, for heavy draught horses on road work, sharpened wedges are also made at the toe, either from existing toe pieces or by welding on "sharps". Although an effective way, the need for removing the shoes is a disadvantage, especially as the wedges soon become blunt and involve further removal and sharpening. This method is rarely used today.

Frost Nails. These sharp hard-headed nails are fitted in place of ordinary nails at the heels, and sometimes toes; or they may be used additionally at the heels on specially wide-fitting shoes, when their shanks are turned over to secure them. They are effective but soon become worn.

Frost or Screw Cogs. These are preferable to frost nails and are easily removed at night, by "taps" or keys, to prevent injury to the horse. They are screwed into specially provided holes in each heel and sometimes also in each toe. When removed, their places should be taken by "blanks" or blunt cogs, to preserve the thread of the holes and prevent burring over of the edges. Various shaped heads are made, and when the chisel-edge type is used, they should lie in the positions described under "Roughing".

The foregoing have disadvantages and consequently have been superseded.

"Mordax" Studs. These, of which many sizes are supplied in tapered, screw and plug types, are designed for easy fitting, to obviate rapid wear and to remain in the shoes until the latter are worn out, and have been proved an excellent non-slipping device. The weight of the horse makes the hard centre pin of the stud sink into the surface thus arresting any slip without jarring. (See illustration.)

Fig. 8   "Mordax" Studs
New and part-worn "Mordax" Studs: the one on the right has had considerable wear but shows the hard "core" which makes it still effective.

Fig. 9   "Mordax" Studs fitted to a shoe

In some instances, no wound can be found. In this case, it is thought that the organism has entered the body from the bowels as a result of damage to the intestinal lining. The normal incubation period is 1–3 weeks, but can be longer. Treatment with antibiotics can be successful if begun as soon as the first signs of stiffness and fever are seen. However, paralysis quickly follows the stiffness and if the disease is not detected until this stage the outcome is more likely to be fatal.

Temporary protection against tetanus (lasting 3–4 weeks) can be gained by administering an injection of Tetanus Antitoxin. To be safe, an unvaccinated horse must be given an injection of Tetanus Antitoxin each and **EVERY** time it gets a cut or wound, no matter how small. To avoid the constant worry of this potentially life-threatening disease, and to save the cost and inconvenience of repeated injections of Tetanus Antitoxin, it is strongly recommended that all horses be permanently immunised. This can be done at any age over three months.

Two primary vaccinations are given with an interval of 4–6 weeks between injections. A booster must be given one year after the second primary vaccination. Thereafter, boosters every second or third year (depending on which particular manufacturer's vaccine is used) will keep the horse permanently protected.

Very young foals are more at risk than adult horses. These are too young to vaccinate. However, they can be protected by vaccinating their dam during the last six weeks of pregnancy, and ensuring that they suckle her first milk (colostrum) during the first 8–12 hours of life to receive its protective antibodies. As an additional precaution, foals can be given an injection of Tetanus Antitoxin when they are two or three days old. This will protect them until they are old enough to be vaccinated.

At this point is it also worthwhile remembering that humans can also contract this serious disease. Since horses can harbour the tetanus organism in their droppings, people working with them may be potentially more at risk than other members of the population. For this reason, anyone involved with horses would be well-advised to ensure that they are vaccinated against tetanus and that their booster vaccinations are kept up-to-date.

'Flu Vaccination. Like human influenza, the equine variety is highly infectious and occurs in epidemics. Although rarely fatal (death can sometimes occur in very young foals), this disease can cause prolonged coughing, lasting weeks or months. Other complications (see page 208) may even affect the horse's health permanently. It is therefore worthwhile trying to protect horses from this disease by vaccination. Unfortunately, vaccination does not always result in complete immunity. Occasionally, during an epidemic, a vaccinated horse may become affected. However, in this case, the symptoms are usually very much milder than in unvaccinated animals.

Because of the high risk of infection being spread at race-meetings, three-day events, shows and other equestrian competitions, the governing bodies organising many of these events have instigated a compulsory vaccination policy for all horses entering them. Thus horses competing in events organised under Jockey Club, F.E.I., or B.H.S. rules must have a "passport" or vaccination certificate completed by a vet which identifies the horse accurately (using both a drawing and a written description of its markings), and a record of the initial 'flu vaccinations and boosters that have been given. If boosters are given at the wrong time or have lapsed, the horse may be ineligible to compete.

If boosters are allowed to lapse, it will be necessary to begin a vaccination course all over again, incurring additional unnecessary expense. The recommended interval between boosters depends on the particular brand of vaccine that has been used, which can be confusing for the horse's owner. Since the correct interval between 'flu boosters must be strictly adhered to in order to comply with compulsory vaccination regulations, the tack room "health planner" can be a great help in ensuring that they are given on time.

A 'flu vaccination course can begin at any age above three months old. Two primary vaccinations are given at an interval of 4–6 weeks. If "Duvaxyn" is used, a booster must be given 6 and 12 months after the second initial injection, and given thereafter at intervals of not more than 12 months. If the other brand currently available, "Prevac", is used, the first booster must be given between 6 and 9 months after the second initial injection, and subsequent boosters must be given at the same interval.

Hackney Horse

For convenience, combined vaccines against both 'flu and tetanus are available. Using this method means that protection against both diseases can be kept up-to-date at the same time. If a 'flu epidemic should occur in the locality it is a sensible precaution to give an extra booster to "top up" protection.

FOOT CARE

Shoes must be removed every 4–6 weeks so that feet can be trimmed and "balanced" to compensate for additional growth. Unshod feet also require trimming at slightly longer intervals to keep them in good shape. Foot care has been described in detail in Chapter 15, page 116.

TEETH CARE

To digest grass or hay effectively, the fibres must first be ground and crushed thoroughly so that the digestive juices and bacteria within the large intestine can work on them. Horses have evolved cheek teeth with hardened surfaces moulded into complex patterns which enable them to do this very efficiently. The constant grinding does, however, result in considerable wear of the surface of the teeth, but unlike human cheek teeth, the equine equivalents continue to erupt through the gums throughout the animal's life so that the worn surface is replaced by "new" tooth from below. Constant wear of opposing teeth should result in a uniform, level surface. In practice, the upper cheek teeth usually lie slightly outside the lower ones, so that the inner edges of the upper teeth and the outer edges of the lower ones are worn more. This means that the outer edges of the upper teeth are worn less, become sharp and cut the cheeks, and the inner edges of the lower ones do the same, but cut the tongue. It is therefore necessary to rasp the teeth from time to time to level their grinding surface, which enables the horse to eat properly, and to remove any sharp projections which may be cutting its mouth.

The usual signs that teeth need attention are the horse's unwillingness to go straight or refusing to take the bit when being ridden, reluctance to eat, dropping partially chewed food from the mouth ("quidding") or the presence of undigested food (particularly fibre) in the droppings. To prevent these problems, an annual dental check up, which includes rasping of the cheek teeth, is recommended for all horses.

Some individual horses may have dental problems which require more frequent attention. These include those that have teeth that do not meet properly. This is most often seen when the first upper cheek tooth lies in front of its lower counterpart. Here, a large unworn "hook" develops at the front of the upper tooth which cuts the cheeks when they are pulled against it by the bit.

Between the ages of 2 and 4 years, young horses lose their temporary cheek teeth and replace them with permanent ones. "Teething" troubles, resulting in lost appetite, are common at this age, and more frequent rasping of the teeth may be necessary to remove sharp edges and keep the animal going to the manger. Likewise, old horses (over 20 years) often suffer problems because of tooth irregularities. Teeth may become loose, or lost altogether, which means that the tooth in the opposite jaw is unworn and becomes sharp. Unlevel, irregular and sharp teeth are a common contributing factor to weight loss in old age. For this reason, more frequent attention is usually required to their teeth. Horses over 20 years old should have a dental check-up every 6 months.

WORMING

Parasitic worms are without doubt the most common cause of ill-health in horses. It has been estimated that over 90% of colic cases are due to current or previous worm damage. Loss of weight, poor appetite, a dull coat and other signs of unthriftiness which are often encountered in horses, are, in many cases, a direct result of worm infestation. Many other forms of ill-health can also be associated with their presence.

All horses acquire worms when they graze. Even when continually stabled, it is almost impossible to rid a horse entirely of worms no matter what treatment is given. This means that regular worm treatment is necessary throughout a horse's life not only to restrict the worm population that it is carrying to a minimum but, equally important, to reduce the risks posed to itself and others by contamination of grazing with worm eggs.

Adult horses appear to develop some degree of partial immunity to worms, enabling them to tolerate low levels of infection without their health being seriously affected. However, small numbers of worms can produce vast numbers of eggs, so that there can be a very rapid build-up of infection in overstocked pastures, and the animal's health will suffer accordingly. Some worms can cause serious damage when only a few are present. In particular, the migrating immature forms of the large redworms (large strongyles) cause extensive damage inside the abdominal cavity, especially to the blood vessels supplying the bowels.

Worming Young Horses. Foals have no immunity to worms and begin picking them up within hours of birth. High levels of infection can quickly build up, and severe illness or death may result if satisfactory worm control measures have not been taken. Often, worm damage occurring during the first twelve months of life results in permanent injury to the bowel which can affect the animal for the rest of its life. Such horses tend to suffer repeated bouts of colic and tend to be chronic "poor doers".

Worm treatment of foals and yearlings is often not as effective as in adult horses, so that frequent worming at intervals of 4–6 weeks (beginning at six weeks of age) is essential for the first two years of life. Other worm control measures are also important when dealing with young stock. These include worming mares in late pregnancy (using a wormer that is recommended for use at this time), scrupulous hygiene in the foaling box, not grazing young stock with older horses, and providing "clean" grazing for mares and foals, that has not had horses on it for twelve months.

Worming Adult Horses. All horses at grass must be wormed regularly. Infective stages of many worms can survive the winter on pastures and are not killed by frosts. Infective larvae, developed from worm eggs laid the previous autumn, are thus on the pasture ready to infect horses turned out in spring. For some unknown reason, worm egg production by the adult female worms in the horse's intestine also increases in the spring (this phenomenon also occurs in stabled horses as well as those at grass). This results in large numbers of the infective stages of worms on the pastures in late spring and early summer. A moderately affected horse has been found to produce in excess of 20 million worm eggs a day, so it is not hard to see how a pasture can become quickly contaminated at this time of year. Regular worming at 4–6 week intervals will help to keep pasture contamination down, but it is important that all horses are wormed at the same time; there is little point in worming just one among a group, as this will not have much effect on pasture contamination. The most important times to worm are late spring (late May to early June) to prevent the summer build-up of worms on the pasture, and late summer (August/September) to prevent an autumn build-up from eggs produced during the summer. Strategic worming at these two times will significantly reduce the level of worm infection of the pasture.

The most effective means of worm control in grazing is

picking up droppings; twice a week in summer, but a longer interval is possible in winter. If it is practical to do this, it is more effective than worming in cutting down pasture contamination. Not over-stocking, harrowing the pasture to break up droppings, resting it and grazing with cattle and sheep are additional measures which can help reduce the risk to horses at grass. Stable manure should never be spread on horse pastures – this poses a very high risk.

Stabled horses also require regular worming. Even though they may not be picking up fresh infection when they do not have access to grazing, they may still have worms present from previous spells at grass, which may be causing damage. Worming every 6–8 weeks should be sufficient.

Choice of Worm Treatment. There are a bewildering variety of drugs available for worm treatment in horses, and it can be very difficult for a horse-owner to know which to choose. Wormers can be divided into the older drugs which only kill the adult worms living in the horse's intestines and are cheaper, and newer drugs which kill all the stages of the worm within the horse but which are more expensive. The older drugs must be given at 4–6 week intervals in order to kill the adult worms that have developed from immature worms already inside the horse but not killed by the previous worm dose. Wormers that kill all stages of the worm's life-cycle can be given at longer intervals (6–8 weeks) which means, in effect, that there is little overall difference in the cost of treatment.

The range of action of wormers also differs, so that some are more effective against particular types of worms than others. Many wormers are not effective against bots or tapeworms. Some have to be used at a different dose rate for different types of worms, so that it is helpful to know the type of worm you are trying to kill. For young stock, a wormer that kills both roundworms and strongyles is adequate for most of the year, but each autumn it is wise to use one that will kill bot and warble larvae. At least once a year, it would also be sensible to use a wormer that kills tapeworms.

Above all, it is important to follow the manufacturers' instructions for each drug very carefully. If there is any doubt about which wormer you should use, the vet is the best person to advise you.

Worms can develop immunity to some types of worm drugs. To avoid this possibility, it is best to use one particular drug for 12 months, and then to change to a completely different type of chemical the next year. Remember that drugs with different trade names may contain the same active ingredient, so check the chemical name, not the trade name.

Checking that a Worm Control Programme is Effective. Not only can worms become immune to some types of worm drugs, but certain individual horses seem to be less responsive to worm treatment than others. It can therefore be helpful to check that a worm control programme is working. This can be done by asking your vet to examine a sample of the animal's droppings. Using a microscope, the number of worm eggs in a gramme of droppings can be counted, giving a good indication of the number of adult egg-laying female worms in the horse's intestines. A "faecal worm egg count" is particularly useful when several horses are grazing together. By testing all the horses at regular intervals (every 2–3 months), it is easy to see whether the contamination of the pasture with worm eggs is being kept down, or whether more frequent worming, or a change to another drug, is necessary. This test only shows evidence of adult worms. It does not reflect the level of immature worms within the horse, as these are not yet laying eggs.

It is often the recently acquired immature worms that are responsible for the more serious effects of parasitic infection when they migrate through their host's tissues. The most injurious of these are the larval stages of the large redworm, strongulus vulgaris, which damage bowel blood vessels and may cause aneurysms (see chapter 22, page 212). Since these particular larvae migrate inside the horse for 6 months and do not become egg-laying adults until 9–10 months after infection, a "faecal egg count" is not much help in detecting their presence, especially in foals.

Recently, a blood test has been developed which can detect changes in some blood proteins caused by worms. This test will detect the presence of immature worms. It can be useful in confirming or ruling out worms as a possible cause of loss of condition, colic or other signs of ill-health which could be associated with worm infection. It can also be used as a reliable check that a worm control programme is satisfactory.

17

BRIDLES, SADDLES AND HARNESS

Riding Bridles. Since the purpose of a bridle is to hold the bit in the horse's mouth, the essential part is the headpiece, which passes over the horse's head and is attached by cheek pieces to the bit. The cheek pieces are sometimes stitched to the bit but buckles or studs are more often used, as these make it easy to take the whole to pieces at any time for cleaning or for changing or renewing any part – this advantage is always forcibly brought home when leather breaks.

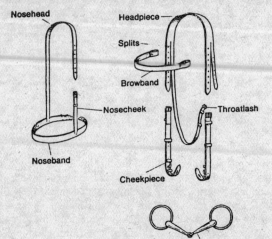

Fig. 10   Parts of a Snaffle Bridle

The headpiece is prevented from slipping forward by the throatlash, which forms part of it and passes around the throat to buckle on the near side. Backward movement is prevented by the browband, which crosses the forehead and has loops at either end through which the headpiece passes.

A noseband is found on most bridles. Although the normal noseband (Cavesson noseband) is purely decorative, a tight noseband fitted below the bit ("drop" noseband) or with tight straps above and below the bit ("grakle" noseband) can be very useful in giving extra control over a difficult horse (those that take a firm hold by opening their mouths or crossing their jaws). All nosebands are held in position by a strap passing through the browband loops and over the poll (under the headpiece) to buckle on the near side. Adjustment of the noseband itself is by a buckle under the jaw.

Bits. We are told there is a key to the mouth of every horse; this is true, but generally the real key is in the hands of the rider, driver or breaker. It is when this key has been "lost" that we have to seek one in the bit. However, horses vary, and the type of bit which will suit one will not suit another; it is usual to try first the snaffle, and if this is found unsuitable – either for control or "balance" – to progress to the double bridle or the Pelham.

The Snaffle. The common form of snaffle is one with a jointed mouthpiece, either "plain" or the less-mild "twisted", with large flat rings either end. Jointed snaffles allow freedom for the tongue but are capable of a painful nutcracker effect on the corners of the mouth. The rings of a standard snaffle can also pinch the skin at the sides of the mouth. For this reason, an egg-butt snaffle is often preferred, as the smooth side-pieces are fixed to the bars of the bit and cannot pinch the mouth. The straight bar snaffle, with the mouthpiece in one complete straight piece of metal, is little seen; it does not allow the same tongue freedom but is without the nutcracker effect of the jointed variety.

For snaffle bits to fit correctly, they should protrude about 0.5cm (¼") on either side of the mouth, and should be adjusted so that they touch the corners of the mouth, just causing the slightest wrinkle in the skin.

The Double Bridle. In this form there are two bits; the bridoon or snaffle and the "bit" or curb, each with its own head piece and reins.

The difference between the bridoon and the ordinary snaffle is one of size. In the former, the mouthpiece (always plain) is finer and the rings smaller and rounded.

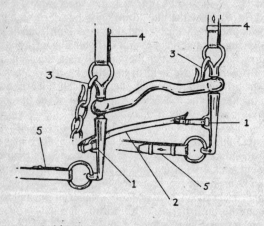

1. Lipstrap eyes
2. Lipstrap
3. Curb chain hooks
4. Cheek straps
5. Bit or Curb reins

Fig. 11 "Weymouth" (Sliding Cheek) Curb Bit of a Double Bridle

The curb bit may be curved upwards to allow space for the tongue. Alternatively, there may be a slight rise in the middle of a straight mouth piece, known as a "port". Curb bits with a port are much more severe and are not generally recommended but are commonly used. When the curb reins are used, pressure is brought on the bars of the mouth and the port rises – thus it will be seen a high port would bear against the roof of the mouth – and a curb chain presses against the chin groove. The cannons, the straight portions either side of the port, extend slightly outside the mouth, where the cheeks of the bit pass through them, forming a swivel which makes them reversible.

The mouthpiece may be twisted on one side, when the smooth surface should lie against the tongue. At the top of the cheeks, small rings are formed to take the head piece and the curb chain hooks. These rings are usually bent slightly outwards, away from the mouth, and this point must be watched for if the bit is reversed. Towards the lower end of each cheek is a small "D" for the lip strap, and at the bottom are the rings for the bit reins.

Double bridles should be adjusted so that the bridoon occupies the position of an ordinary snaffle, the bit lying very slightly below it so that it does not contact the corners of the lips. The curb chain, looped on to the offside hook, is passed *outside* the bridoon and twisted to the right, link by link from that side, so that it lies flat, and is then placed on the nearside hook, again outside the bridoon, at a length which will allow two fingers to be placed edgeways between it and the jaw. It is often advised that the end link should be hooked on first and then the chain shortened to the correct length by following with the appropriate link. In practice it may be found easier to adjust the length first, putting the link on with the thumb uppermost, then looping the last link on top. Curb chains are always far too long, even allowing for the different lengths required, and if you do not have superfluous links removed, neatness can be obtained by hooking up an extra link or two on the offside first to make it even. Do not make the mistake of buying a fine, thin chain with the idea that it is kinder – it is not; a thin chain cuts more easily than a heavy one.

A free "fly-link" will be found running on the centre of the curb chain, and by making your chain even, as recommended, this *will* lie in the centre. Through this fly-link the lip strap is passed and buckled on the near side. One purpose of the lip strap is to prevent the horse taking hold of the cheek of the bit with his lower lip; this would otherwise happen in some cases, but a better reason is to avoid the loss of the chain when unbridling or carrying. Chains should, of course, be undone only on the near side when unbridling, but may become detached. Therefore, use a lip strap and keep it buckled when carrying the bridle.

Pelham. The Pelham resembles the bit of the double bridle, and can be regarded as a combination of curb bit and bridoon. An additional large ring is provided at the mouthpiece on either cheek for the bridoon reins, which are usually referred to as "cheek reins" in this bridle.

In the mouth, the Pelham should occupy the position of the curb. In other respects the remarks under "Double Bridle" apply, except that it is common to pass the curb chain through both bridoon rings.

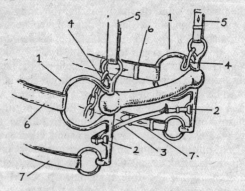

1. Bridoon cheek rings
2. Lip strap eyes
3. Lip strap
4. Curb chain hooks
5. Cheek straps
6. Bridoon, Snaffle or Cheek reins
7. Bit or Curb reins

Fig. 12 "Mullen-mouth" Pelham

An excellent type of Pelham is that with a slight upward curve in a smooth mouthpiece, in place of the port – the "Mullen-mouth" Pelham. The advantages of the port are obtained without its disadvantage of possible severity.

Riding Saddles. Saddles are for the comfort of the rider *and the horse* – bareback riding is eventually injurious to the horse's back by bringing weight on the spine instead of on the muscles either side. That being so, the first requirement of any saddle is obvious: even distribution of weight over the back muscles.

The distribution of weight must not be extended as far back as the loins, which are a comparatively weak part of the horse's anatomy, nor as far forward as to interfere with the play of the shoulders. Too broad a saddle will bear upon the spine and withers, causing pressure sores ("saddle galls"), whilst a narrow one will pinch. There should always be a clear channel along the horse's spine, when viewed from behind, with a rider in the saddle.

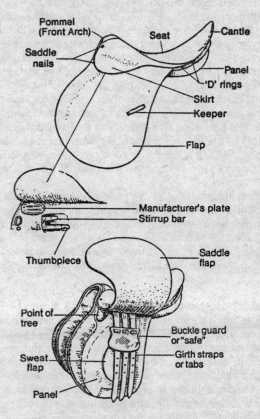

Fig. 13 Parts of the Saddle

A well-fitting, general-purpose saddle is suitable for hacking and general riding, and is best for anyone just starting to ride. However, different forms of riding call for different riding positions (seats), so that various types of saddles have been specially developed to suit them. Thus, racing, show-jumping, dressage, eventing and showing all have their own distinctive shape of saddle.

It is important to buy a correctly-fitting saddle. Often, a saddle appears to fit well when placed on the horse's back and it is not until someone actually sits on it that it can be seen to be a bad fit. Saddle sizes are usually measured in inches, but the cut can vary considerably, so that the size is not sufficient to ensure a good fit. (The same-sized saddle could equally well be cut to suit someone with short legs and a large seat or someone else with long legs and a small seat.)

Being the most expensive item of tack, it is worthwhile taking trouble to ensure that the saddle fits both you and your horse, and the best person to give this advice is a reputable saddler – preferably one who is a member of the Worshipful Company of Saddlers. In many instances, a good second-hand saddle of a reputable make is a better buy than some of the cheaper new ones.

In time, the stuffing in the panels becomes flattened and insufficient and permits injurious pressure. If the remedy of restuffing is not immediately possible, a folded blanket may be placed under the saddle but should always be lifted clear of the spine and withers when girthing up, and should always be smooth, unwrinkled and free from any adhering "foreign bodies".

Numnahs. These are saddle-shaped pads of man-made fibres, sheepskin or felt which are sometimes fitted beneath the saddle to prevent pressure sores. If the saddle no longer fits properly because the stuffing in the panels has become flattened and insufficient, the best solution is to have it restuffed, rather than relying on a numnah. Care must always be taken, when fitting a numnah under a saddle, to ensure that its front end fits well up into the arch of the saddle, otherwise it may produce pressure on the withers.

Girths. Many materials are used for girths including leather, webbing, nylon and "string". Leather girths are good if they are well cared for but can be dangerous if allowed to become hard. They can sometimes cause chafing ("girth galls") in thin-skinned animals but a girth sleeve of sheepskin or other material can be fitted to prevent this. Webbing girths are seldom used nowadays, as they are not easy to clean, tend to rot and can therefore be dangerous. Nylon girths are very satisfactory and easy to clean. Multi-strand nylon ("string") girths are specially popular, as they are the least likely to cause chafing, and they are easily washed and dried.

DRIVING HARNESS

The parts of driving harness are shown in the diagram on page 150.

CORRECT FITTING

Collars. Neck collars must fit well and evenly to the shoulders without rubbing, but at the same time they must not be tight and difficult to place, nor must they bear on the neck in front of the withers. It should be possible to insert between the neck and collar: (1) At the top – the flat of the hand. (2) At any part of the sides – the flat of the fingers. (3) At the bottom – the hand and wrist.

Except at the top of the neck, in front of the withers, where galling results from pressure, collar injuries arise from *friction* due to the movement of the shoulder blades. Relief from injuries is best effected by narrower or wider fitting collars, not by the use of pads or chambering (removal of stuffing over an injured part).

The collar is shaped so that it must be turned upside down to pass over the head, then reversed when beyond the ears. Beginners have been noticed trying to put a collar on the wrong way up.

The Hames. The hames are the collar-shaped metal branches in the space between the fore- and afterwale of the collar. If they are not shaped perfectly to the collar, the fit of the latter is

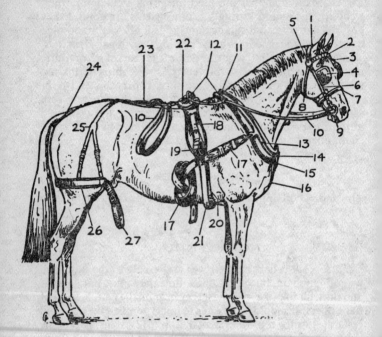

1. Headpiece
2. Browband
3. Blinker stays
4. Blinker or Winker
5. Rosette
6. Cheekpiece
7. Noseband
8. Throatlash
9. Liverpool bit
10. Reins
11. Hame strap
12. Terrets
13. Hames
14. Hame strap (or chain)
15. Collar
16. False martingale
17. Trace
18. Back band
19. Tug (shaft)
20. Girth
21. Belly band
22. Pad or Saddle
23. Back (Crupper) strap
24. Crupper
25. Loin strap
26. Breeching
27. Breeching strap

Fig. 14   Single Driving Harness

upset. They carry the trace bar, and the driving rings for the reins.

Hame Strap or Chain. The purpose of this strap is to bring the sides of the collar together at the top. It must be regularly examined, as stretching allows the collar to open slightly leading to pinching of the neck.

The Pad or Saddle. Like all saddles, this must not bear upon the backbone, and must be kept steady by the girth – which should not be so tight that a finger cannot be inserted between it and the belly. The Belly Band, a continuation of the Back Band supporting the shaft tugs, must have two hands breadth between itself and the belly.

The Crupper. The Crupper is connected to the Saddle by a Back or Crupper Strap. Its purpose is to prevent forward movement of the saddle and should therefore be no tighter or looser than necessary for this.

Breeching. The Breeching should be only slightly above the level of the shafts and hang horizontally. Adjustment is by the Loin Strap. Its fitting is important: although it must not allow the Saddle to be pushed forward when going downhill or backing, it must not interfere with the movement of the quarters; at other times there should be about four inches beween the buttocks and the Breeching (when the horse has his weight in the Collar).

Traces. These should be hooked into the trace attachment at a length which keeps the horse clear of the footboard of the vehicle at all times.

Bridle. The remarks under Riding Bridles apply generally. Single bits are used, usually the Liverpool Driving Bit, shown in the diagram, or the double-ringed snaffle which is familiar to everyone. In double harness, that is, for two horses side-by-side, the "Buxton" bit is often seen; this has an additional metal bar between the two cheeks to prevent a rein becoming entangled with the pole. When Blinkers are worn, they must allow free vision forward without being loose and flapping, the width being adjusted by the Blinker Stays on the forehead. The avowed object of Blinkers is to prevent the horse seeing the following wheels, but it would seem we have another example of die-hard custom; Blinkers were not part of Army draught horses' equipment, and nothing was lost in the way of safe driving – or appearance – but, of course, these horses were properly broken to harness work.

HARNESSING-UP

The Collar is put on first, usually with Hames and Traces attached, the latter loosely knotted out of harm's way. It is turned upside down until the ears are passed, but widening may be necessary first by stretching on the knee or a bracket. The Housing Strap must be kept as tight as possible.

Next follow the Saddle, Crupper and Breeching. The Saddle is placed slightly *behind* its correct position until the Crupper has been passed over the tail into place; it is then adjusted and girthed up, but the Belly Band is left unbuckled.

The Bridle is now put on, the reins passed through the Terrets and fastened to the bit, the spare end being folded through the near Terret.

Putting-to. Stand the horse in front of the vehicle, raise the shafts above his back and pull the cart forward; lower and run the shafts through the Tugs as far as the stops. Hook in the Traces and buckle the Breeching around them to the slots on the shafts. Finally, adjust the Belly Band.

Unharnessing. When taking a horse out of the shafts, the Traces should be undone last as many animals "make a dash" as soon as these are unfastened. The rest of the gear can then be removed in the stable in the normal way, though most people prefer to slip the bridle off before leading in.

BALANCE OF TWO—WHEELED VEHICLES

To ease the horse, care should be taken to preserve the balance of a two-wheeled vehicle by careful placing of the load – the sliding seat simplifies this. Over-weighting in front forces the shafts down and throws weight on the horse through the saddle, whilst the reverse exerts an upward pull on him. Correctly balanced, there is slight play of the shafts, and gentle up and down movement of the shaft tug buckle at the trot.

CARE OF TACK

The condition of tack, that is, saddles, bridles, etc., collectively, is a sure guide to the standard of stable-management. A high polish on tack looks very smart, but is unnecessary except in patent leather work on harness; what counts is its condition – cleanliness and suppleness.

When dealing with leather parts, undo all buckles and then wash off grease with *warm* water, dry and vigorously rub in saddle soap. For leather panels and girths, sweat flaps, girth tabs and the underside of flaps, there is little better than neatsfoot oil for suppleness and preservation. On the seat and the outside of flaps, the saddle soap must be well worked in to avoid soiling clothes, but these parts should not be polished. For black harness, special "harness polish" is obtainable. When cleaning girth tabs and stirrup leathers notice should be made of any wear at the holes, and at the parts of the leathers passing through the stirrup irons or over the spring bar. Wear may be reduced by occasionally varying the length of stirrup used, and by raising the girth a hole on one side and lowering on the other. Buckles also should be cleaned and wiped with an oily rag. When buckled bridles are used, do not neglect the leather which takes the wear of the bit rings.

Linen or serge lined saddles and collars should be thoroughly brushed regularly, or it may be necessary to sponge them lightly to remove grease, using the minimum of water. Carefully scraping with a blunt knife, followed by brushing, is a good method of removing grease.

Bits and stirrup irons are usually made of stainless steel. These can be washed with warm water and polished using metal polish and a cloth. When cleaning the bit, polish should only be used on the cheek-pieces, never on the mouth-piece, because of the very unpleasant taste of metal polish.

18

MARE AND FOAL

There is great satisfaction in breeding from one's own mare and rearing and handling the youngster. However, breeding and rearing entail a lot of work, some additional facilities, and the expenses incurred are often more than the value of the progeny of such an enterprise. It should not be undertaken without serious consideration. Some knowledge of what to expect is essential.

For those embarking on horsebreeding for the first time, it may be preferable to send the mare to a stud to be covered and to return her there to foal, on this occasion – concentrating their efforts on looking after the pregnant mare and raising the foal, before undertaking the responsibility of foaling the mare at home next time.

The most important question is whether the mare is really suitable for breeding – whether she is healthy and of suitable temperament and conformation. Unfortunately, some mares that are unable to be ridden, because of lameness or for some other reason, are sometimes put in foal, when they are totally unsuitable.

Stallions are licensed in the U.K., so defects in that quarter need not be feared. Selecting a stallion requires careful thought. Wherever possible, it is best to go and take a close look at all those that are standing locally, before deciding. As far as possible, the sire should balance any bad points in the mare, but the best guide is the stock he has been getting. If a stallion cannot be found locally, the Stud Books of the appropriate Breed Society, the Hunter Improvement & National Light Horse Breeding Society, or the National Pony Society, as well as the advertisement columns of "horsy" periodicals, offer plenty of choice.

The Age for Breeding. Fillies can be put to the stallion as young as two years old, but they are very immature at this age. Normally, this is not done until they are four, so that they foal for the first time at five when they are fully mature. Mares will go on breeding well into their twenties, particularly if they have had a foal each year. They are unlikely to conceive if breeding for the first time is left until they are over 15 years.

The Best Time for Breeding. Except during winter, when they show no sexual behaviour, mares usually have a season (oestrous) which lasts from 2–5 days and recurs 16 days after the end of the previous season – i.e. approximately a 3-week cycle. The mare normally ovulates 24 hours before the end of her season, and this is the optimum time for mating with a stallion.

In selecting the month for service, we should consider the foal. Obviously the best time for the youngster to make its appearance is when the weather is mild and the grass at its best, so that it has a good start in life; this points to May. Therefore, the average gestation period being 11 months, the ideal time for service is June.

Pregnancy Tests. It is helpful for all concerned to know whether or not a mare has conceived, and there are a variety of ways in which this can be done. By means of an ultrasound scanner, pregnancy can sometimes be detected as early as 12 days after covering. However, this examination is not usually performed until 3–4 weeks, when it gives very accurate results. A vet can usually detect pregnancy with accuracy by manual examination of the mare's womb, through her rectum, from six weeks onwards. Blood tests can be performed between 8 and 14 weeks, and urine tests from 5 months onwards, although these are not always 100% reliable.

CARE OF THE IN-FOAL MARE

During pregnancy, a certain amount of exercise is necessary to keep the mare healthy. A pregnant mare can be ridden quite safely for the first six months but after this, riding is not advisable. Usually, in-foal mares obtain sufficient exercise if they are turned out, but if they have to be stabled for any reason, they should be led out for gentle walking exercise.

The following is a suggested timetable:-

The last three months. Although some mares show obvious abdominal enlargement during the last three months, some will show no outward signs at all. The most reliable sign of approaching parturition is swelling of the udder, which is usually noticeable in the last six weeks of pregnancy. At the same time, mares will usually "wax up", producing a wax-like secretion which can drip from the teats in the days prior to foaling. Most of the growth of the foal occurs in the last three months, and some supplementary feeding, in the form of a high protein concentrate, will be required during this stage. Plenty of good grass will keep the mare healthy and help milk production, and she should be turned out for increasing periods daily.

The last month. A comfortable, roomy and well-bedded loose-box should be provided for foaling time, and the mare should be sleeping in this now. It is essential that this box should be of ample size to allow free movement and to offer no risk of casting. Five square metres (16 sq ft) is ideal for horses, but smaller boxes can be used for ponies. If the box is too large, it may be cold. It should be well ventilated but draught-free, and should be well lit, so that it is always possible to see what is going on. It should be scrupulously clean – having been washed and disinfected thoroughly before any bedding is put down. A deep bed of good-quality straw is the best bedding for a foaling box, and this must be kept clean at all times, and soiled portions renewed immediately. A means of observing without disturbing the mare should be arranged in the box, as the less an animal is interfered with at these times, the better.

Towards the end of the month, feeding must be such as to avoid constipation, and an occasional bran mash is useful.

Foaling day. The more natural the conditions under which the mare has been kept, the less trouble there will be at this time. Foaling is usually straightforward, and fussing must be avoided. The amateur should, however, have an experienced person present, as unless the attendant understands fully what assistance may be required he is likely to do more harm than good. The ideal person is someone who works on a stud and is used to dealing with foaling mares.

Foaling. Foaling begins with the onset of contractions of the womb (uterus), which is known as first stage labour. The mare becomes restless and uncomfortable, moving around the box, and often "sweats up". There may be false alarms, with uncomfortable bouts during the last weeks of pregnancy, due to discomfort caused by the position of the foal.

The duration of the first stage labour varies considerably but is usually around 3–4 hours. The onset of second stage labour is indicated by the rupture of the outer layer of foetal membranes within the womb, releasing its fluid contents – often known as "breaking water". This is shortly followed by the appearance of the foetal sac (in which the foal will be born), and straining commences. Mares usually lie down to strain more effectively but often get up and down and change position during this stage.

The normal presentation in which foals are born is with both forelegs extended and the head lying on the knees. As straining increases, the first foot appears within the sac, with the second slightly behind it. The head should then follow, requiring maximum effort from the mare to push this out. The chest follows quickly and a final expulsive effort is required to pass the hips, after which straining ceases, and the mare may lie with the foal's hind legs still in her vagina for some while.

Second stage labour is extremely rapid in the mare – ranging from 5–60 minutes and averaging around 20 minutes. If a mare has been straining for 30 minutes and nothing (no membrane or foot) has appeared, a vet should be called immediately. If an experienced assistant is available, he or she should insert a hand that has been washed, disinfected and lubricated, to see if there is some abnormality of presentation (i.e. whether a head and two fore feet can be felt) or whether the head or feet can carefully be adjusted into position.

Mares rarely have problems foaling; when they do, the foal often dies as a result. It is important to know what should happen and to take prompt action when something does not happen. Anyone assisting must know exactly what they are doing, and this is why it is best for the inexperienced to send a mare to a stud to foal or to have an experienced stud groom available to supervise the birth.

When the foal is born, it must be seen that it is free of the foetal membranes and able to breathe. If, even although not so encumbered, the youngster does not begin to breathe, efforts must be made to encourage the action of the lungs by slapping the sides or by pressing at regular intervals on the hinder ribs and the belly. When there is no trouble, the foal will be up and sucking half-an-hour after its delivery.

Although the umbilical cord often breaks naturally during birth or is subsequently bitten through by the mare, as in nature, no attempt should be made to sever the cord soon after birth because blood is being squeezed from the membranes by the womb contraction, and cutting the cord will deprive the foal of this blood. Occasionally, a very tough cord may remain attached, and this can be tied 5–10cm (2″–4″) from the navel before cutting it. The umbilical stump should be treated with iodine or antibiotic powder to prevent bacteria entering, which may cause joint-ill or septicaemia. Soiled bedding must be removed for burning, and renewed.

The dam should be left alone, if all is well with her, until she has licked the foal, after which she can be given a small feed. If she does not dry the foal sufficiently it may be necessary to do so, using a cloth or clean straw.

The mare's womb continues to contract and should expel the foetal membranes soon after foaling. If these have not been passed by 24 hours after the birth, a vet should be called to remove them. It is important that all the membranes are passed because if small portions are retained, infection of the womb, with possible serious consequences, may result. A good stud groom will be able to tell by looking at the membranes whether or not a piece is missing.

As a final note on this subject, it might be pointed out that, in the usual contrary way of animals, mares often choose the most unexpected time to produce their offspring – not infrequently the one moment when the observer has decided he can be spared.

CARE OF MARE AND FOAL

After foaling. A normal foal should be standing within two hours of birth, and should have suckled within four hours. Foals receive no antibodies from their dam before birth. High levels of antibodies are concentrated in the dam's honey-like first milk (colostrum). The foal's digestive system is only capable of absorbing these antibodies for a short while (8–12 hours) after birth, so it is vital for the foal to receive colostrum during this period, as this is the only source of antibodies to protect it from the many infectious agents which it will encounter during the first months of its life. Thus if a foal has not sucked by 6–8 hours, the mare must be milked and colustrum fed by bottle, or if the foal will not suck at all, it must be given by the vet, by stomach tube.

After foaling, both mare and foal should stay in the box for a few days, and may then be let out for an hour or two each day in good weather. Food should still be of a laxative nature – plenty of green meal and occasional bran mashes.

Tetanus can strike young foals, and for this reason they are often given an injection of tetanus antitoxin during the first week of life to provide temporary protection, as they should not be vaccinated until three months old.

Four weeks. By four weeks the foal will have learned to nibble grass by imitating its mother, and will learn to eat other feeds when fed with her. Ideally, a creep feed (a special high protein ration to which only the foal has access) should be introduced from 3–4 months of age. The more gradually the foal's digestive system can adapt to the change in its diet from milk, the better (and the less will be the setback which can accompany weaning).

Whenever possible, the foal should become accustomed to being led in a foaling slip (a small head collar). Doing this at an early age makes leading and handling much easier later on.

Weaning. A mare's milk starts to decline in quantity and quality after six months, so it is usual to wean foals at between six and eight months old. By the time of weaning, the foal should have been accustomed to a creep feed for some time.

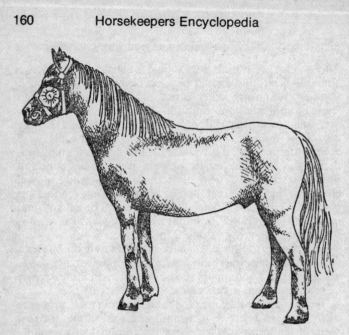

Dartmoor Pony

Ideally, it is best to wean a batch of mares and foals together at grass, by removing one mare from the group each day, keeping these mares well away out of earshot. If this is not possible, it will be necessary to confine the foal to a box for several days. Here again, if another foal can be weaned at the same time, the company provided will make the experience less traumatic.

The mare's feed will have to be cut back for a few days to help her milk dry up. If she is still producing large amounts of milk, it may be necessary to ease the pressure by milking out a little for a day or two. After weaning, a close watch should be kept on the mare's udder for signs of infection (mastitis) – a hot painful udder, with clots in the milk, and a mare that is off her food and may have a temperature.

A foal will always be happier in the company of another, and liberal feeding at this stage is important. An hour or two's exercise at grass can be allowed each day, but opportunities should not be missed to handle and lead youngsters whenever possible.

Exercise, good feeding and shelter, especially in the first winter, are all-important in giving the animal a good start in life; ground lost now is not easily recovered.

Preparation for breaking. Regular handling from the beginning, as already suggested, greatly simplifies the task of breaking, in fact it forms the first lessons. The voice is of immense value and the foal soon learns to obey simple commands such as "stand", "walk", etc., during leading exercise. "Steady" is possibly the most useful word in the horseman's vocabulary, in or out of stables. The dam is an excellent teacher, by example, while the two are still together. A horse already "broken to voice" will be little trouble in breaking to work.

Remember, too, it is essential to have the youngster's confidence; strictly fair, *deserved* correction is quickly understood and appreciated as such whilst the reverse is resented and results in sullenness or bad temper. Particularly is this so in teaching "stable manners". Teach the foal to "move over" and "stand" when told, and accustom it to being stroked all over in preparation for grooming, and to have its feet picked up for grooming and shoeing. The padded pole (see page 73) is useful when this stroking is violently objected to, but gentle persistence is more effective.

The owner will now, if ever, realise the importance of selecting a *good* farrier; the feet will have to be trimmed regularly, and for this we need a man who not only knows his job thoroughly but goes about it quietly and with an even temper – and without nervousness. The right farrier is, indeed, a valued assistant in these first breaking lessons.

By gaining the foal's confidence now, future training is made easy and the character of the horse-to-be is formed.

19

HEALTH AND DISEASE

The objects of this section are to enable the horsekeeper, firstly, to eliminate avoidable trouble; secondly, to recognise immediately the first signs of ill-health so that treatment may be applied in the early stages, when it is most effective, thirdly, to co-operate with his vet either by intelligent assistance or, at least, by not increasing his difficulties.

No suggestion is made that treatment of any but the least serious complaints and injuries should be attempted by the layman. It is foolish for an amateur to interfere on the strength of only vague knowledge of veterinary matters, or to experiment with patent "cure-alls" of the composition and effects of which he is ignorant. The only humane and economic way is to obtain the services of an expert, qualified person. He can, however, ease the professional's task by supplying all relevant information, by having the necessary facilities such as a bridle, water, soap and towel, etc. to hand, and by carrying out instructions as requested.

The Veterinary Surgeon, unlike the doctor, is handicapped from the beginning in that he must discover for himself such facts as will enable him accurately to diagnose, without verbal assistance from his patient.

First Signs of Trouble. Ill-health can be recognised by any departure from the normal appearance and behaviour.

Unless any of the following are normal in the particular animal, they should be regarded with suspicion: unusual attitude or stance; reluctance to get up or move; dullness and a tendency to mope and avoid companions; changed appetite; "tight" skin or harsh "staring" coat; unusual breathing; marked uneasiness; excessive sweating; abnormality in the droppings. These are only general indications. To diagnose the particular trouble they must be linked up with specific symptoms or known conditions.

When any of these signs are noticed, examine the horse carefully. It may be a trivial matter which you can put right yourself. If the horse is lying down, do not immediately rush to the 'phone, he may only be resting. The vet is a busy person, and it is unfair to him and other people in charge of animals to call him out unnecessarily; attention to a more serious case may be delayed through his absence.

If you decide attention is necessary, note everything you can about the case that may be of assistance to the vet in forming his opinion as to its urgency, the treatment likely to be necessary, and the drugs and equipment he will need to bring. With this information he may also be able to give advice over the telephone for emergency treatment until his arrival.

When he arrives, be ready for him and give him all the known *facts*, even apparently trivial ones may be useful, but remember he will not be interested in your theories.

For his inspection he may require your help in various ways.

To Get a Horse Up. It is usually ineffective to try to coax a horse up. Put on his headcollar (this gives you more control than a halter), and with a jerk on the rope call him sharply. Be sure there is plenty of bedding under his feet, to avoid slipping, stand well away and give him room so that he does not hit himself or you when scrambling to his feet.

Holding for Examination. This is done in a similar way to leading in or out of the stable. Stand in front of the horse and facing him, with a hand either side of the head-collar or bridle. While the hindquarters are being examined, it is often advisable, to prevent kicking, to hold up a forefoot. Run your hand down the back tendons to the fetlock joint, press, and speak to the horse, then just let the toe of the foot rest on your fingers when he has lifted it.

"Trotting-up". You may be asked to "trot the horse up", that is, to trot it away from the examiner, back towards him, and then past him. It is best to use a bridle to do this, as it gives better

control than a headcollar or halter. The reins should be taken
over the horse's head and held on the near side on a loose rein –
being held at least 30–45cm (12″–18″) from the bit, so that head
movement is not restricted in any way. Look where you are
going, not at the horse, and if you have difficulty in making him
trot do not pull at him, he must be driven forward by an
assistant. When turning, unless you have been told otherwise,
stop and turn to the right so that you do not obscure the
examiner's view. Usually, turns have to be made sharply, with
the hindlegs as a pivot.

GENERAL SYMPTOMS

These serve as a guide in diagnosis, and any one of them in
conjunction with one or more others, may indicate the ailment.
Similarly, the absence of a symptom is useful in eliminating the
possibility of a particular complaint.

Temperature. The normal temperature of a horse is 38°C
(100.5°F), but it can vary between 37.7 and 38.3°C (100 and
101°F). The temperature is taken by inserting the thermometer
into the rectum for at least one minute. When the temperature
has to be taken on several consecutive days, this should be done
at the same time each day. A horse's temperature normally
rises slightly during the day, and is at its lowest in the morning.
A horse with a temperature of over 38.8°C (102°F) can be
considered to have a fever and should receive veterinary
attention.

Infectious diseases are always accompanied by a rise in
temperature, which is often the first symptom. It is a wise
precaution, therefore, to separate an animal "with a temperature" from the others, and to take steps to avoid carrying the
infection or contagion to healthy animals.

An infectious disease is one which can be spread indirectly,
usually by the breath, whilst contagion is spread by contact,
directly or indirectly. Both are frequently used loosely and
considered interchangeable, and many diseases are both
infectious and contagious.

For general treatment of fever, the instructions under "Food
& Water" on page 169 should be followed, and in the early

stages a mild laxative is of value – a dose of from 15–85 gms
($\frac{1}{2}$–3 oz) of Glauber or Epsom Salts, according to age and size,
in the food or water, is recommended.

Pulse. It is not easy to detect changes in the pulse, but it can be
felt with the first two fingers where the submaxillary artery
crosses the lower jaw, at the inside of the elbow or immediately
above the fetlock. The rate is normally about 35–40 per minute,
being faster in feverish conditions, and slower in debility.

Appetite. Generally, the horse is a greedy feeder, always ready
for a meal, and a poor appetite is suspicious. Distinction must
be made between loss of appetite and inability or difficulty in
eating; most horses will make valiant attempts to eat, even with
obstruction or injury in the mouth or throat.

Refusing food may be due to overwork, or to impaction of
the bowels (constipation). The latter is a common problem in
stabled horses and is usually accompanied by hard droppings.
Although laxative mashes are frequently given to prevent this,
once impaction occurs it may require stronger laxatives to be
given by a vet, by stomach tube, to bring relief.

Difficulty in eating, and "quidding" – allowing food to drop
out of the mouth after an attempt to chew – may indicate
trouble with the teeth, injury or obstruction in the mouth or
throat, or soreness.

An abnormal or depraved appetite is frequently noticed
when worms are present, or in indigestion. It may be due to
"vice", such as crib-biting – gnawing woodwork, etc.

Refusing to drink is often simply due to some objection to
the water or container – dirt or odour.

Attitude. Normally the horse stands with the forefeet planted
firmly and squarely, but frequently rests a hindfoot.

Resting or "pointing" a forefoot, that is, placing it in
advance of the other when standing, usually on the toe, is to
relieve it of weight and indicates trouble in that foot, possibly
due to pus in the foot or some other very painful condition. If
there is trouble in both fore feet – as happens in laminitis
(inflammation of the sensitive lining of the hoof wall), both feet
are placed well forward. When the forelegs are held wide apart,

it is usually a sign of chest affection. Continual pawing and scraping with the toe may be because of disease of the navicular bone, or just a general manifestation of pain (e.g. in colic).

If the hindfeet are drawn well forward and there is reluctance to back, suspect trouble in those feet.

Inability to rise follows tetanus (lockjaw), sprained back muscles, spinal injury, etc.

General uneasiness, constantly lying down and getting up again, is often the result of stomach pains (colic, for example) and when these are severe, the symptom is accompanied by quick, laboured breathing.

Constant stamping, or rubbing one leg against the other, is often caused by the invasion of mites giving rise to irritation. The condition is sometimes called "itchy heels" and is more often found in heavy draught horses with much feathering on the legs.

An unusual amount of scratching, biting, and rubbing against trees or other convenient hard objects, should lead to an inspection for insects, such as lice, which are common in winter and early spring. In summer, rubbing the mane and tail is more likely to be due to "sweet itch" – an allergy to the bites of a certain type of midge.

Breathing. The respirations may be judged by watching or feeling the rise and fall of the flanks, and by the expiration of breath from the nostrils. When at rest, the breathing should be noiseless, steady and even, the normal respirations being about 10–15 per minute.

Breathing sounds usually point to affections of the nose, throat or lungs.

Quickened breathing is present in most chest complaints and when in conjunction with general uneasiness is a sign of great pain, as in severe colic.

Painful breathing may be looked for in pleurisy.

Doubled expirations, that is, with two separate efforts, means that the horse is suffering from a lung problem caused by an allergy to moulds from fodder or bedding (COPD).

Excreta. The droppings should be passed in small balls which break on the ground, golden brown in stable-fed, greenish in grass-fed horses. If they are too hard or soft, digestive disturbance is to be suspected. From a microscopic examination of a sample of droppings, worms or their eggs can be detected.

The urine is rather thick and yellow in health, but has a bright colour when there is fever.

Membranes. The visible membranes, the linings of the eyes, nose and mouth, should be pink and moist. There is a yellowish tinge in liver complaints; paleness in anaemia; reddening and dryness in fever, and a purple tinge in shock.

Skin and coat. The skin should be supple and elastic, and the coat should lie flat and smooth, with a certain amount of gloss. When any of these qualities are missing it is usually a sign that the horse is ill or off-colour (malnutrition, worms, dehydration and so on). The coat will, of course, "stare" or stand up when the animal is cold, but apart from this, may be a warning of worms. A scurfy coat, if not through lack of grooming, may be caused by a skin disease.

Excessive sweating, unless due to weather conditions or hard work, often results from general weakness but is sometimes a symptom of great pain or tetanus.

20

NURSING OF
SICK HORSES

The general management of sick animals is an important part of their treatment and has great effect on speed of recovery and subsequent restoration to full strength and fitness.

Stabling and Exercise. In favourable weather the paddock makes the best sick-bay for most cases. A run at grass provides three essentials: unlimited fresh air, sunlight and natural food, together with gentle exercise which the animal can regulate to his own particular requirements.

When weather conditions or the particular ailment make stabling necessary, ample ventilation without draughts must be assured. Bedding should be plentiful and fulfil all requirements, being dry, clean, elastic and level, to encourage proper rest. Quiet is essential in all cases, but particularly in nervous diseases, when it may be advisable to darken the windows. In serious illness it should be the rule that no-one but the person in charge of the patient is allowed in or near the box, whether or not there is risk of carrying infection; this will eliminate at least some unnecessary disturbance and noise.

The need for meticulous cleaning of the stable, feeding and water bowls, and tack, clothing or grooming kit used on a horse with an infectious disease cannot be over-emphasised. Some diseases, such as strangles, can easily be spread by discharges, while skin diseases, such as ringworm, can be picked up through rugs, tack or grooming kits contaminated with spores. If possible, a special "sick box", should be available, where a horse with an infectious condition can be isolated and looked after by one person only. Ideally, this box should have concrete walls, which are easier to clean and disinfect thoroughly afterwards than a wooden one. Steam cleaning is the best way of cleaning the box afterwards, but a thorough wash with a strong effective disinfectant is also usually satisfactory, especially if the box is left empty for a time.

Food and Water. It is in dealing with sickness that a horsekeeper's claim to be a "good feeder" is most severely tested.

Whilst the concentrate ration should be reduced according to the duration of illness, every effort must be made to keep up condition. The best hay obtainable will form most of the diet and it will usually be of value to include some bran, but the value of green fodder and roots must not be overlooked. It is very necessary to keep the bowels in good order, and fresh green food is ideally suited for this as well as being acceptable to the poorest appetite which needs tempting. Linseed and bran mashes, gruel, etc., will be found useful.

Certain principles must be observed: small quantities of the most easily digested food are to be given at frequent, regular intervals. No uneaten food is to be left in the stable in the hope that the horse may eat it in time – he will not; since it becomes tainted with his own saliva and with unavoidable odours, he will soon lose any appetite he had. Feeding cannot be forced. A poor appetite may be tempted by offering variety, particularly in debility, and the addition of a sweetener, such as molasses, is often a means of making a food more attractive and of encouraging the appetite. When there is disturbance of the digestive system, good results may follow from withholding food for several hours – this might be recommended also for humans.

Clean water should always be available, but it must be renewed frequently as, like other food, it soon becomes tainted. In cold weather it may, with advantage, have the chill taken off.

Clothing and bandages. The temperature must be regulated to avoid extremes, and the best way of maintaining body warmth without denying fresh air is by clothing, which can be reduced or increased as circumstances demand. Over-clothing must be avoided; to a weak animal heavy rugs can be tiring and may further weaken him by causing sweating. Carefully observe all the rules of rugging-up: comfortable fitting, no interference with movement or breathing, and no chafing. In summer, light linen "summer sheets" will be found an advantage as protection from flies.

Bandages may be necessary for warmth or other purposes, and, again, the rules must be strictly followed: no tightness to interfere with the circulation or with movement, and they must be rolled on evenly. They should be removed at intervals during the day, and the limbs rubbed to improve circulation before replacing. Woollen bandages are best, and if less elastic material is used, a layer of cotton wool should be placed underneath, with special attention to joints and swollen parts.

Whether wounds need bandaging or not will depend on a variety of factors. In the early stages, a bandage may be necessary to keep the wound clean and to prevent swelling around it. Later on, a pressure bandage may be needed to prevent the formation of excessive amounts of granulation

Highland Pony

tissue, which is often known as "proud flesh". In other cases, when the wound is clean and dry, with no swelling or "proud flesh" formation, it may be left exposed to the air, which will aid healing and scab formation. Wounds over moving parts may need bandages to restrict movement or to keep ointment in place, and prevent the repeated drying and cracking which so often delays healing in areas such as the back of the pastern.

The vet will usually advise whether or not a wound needs bandaging, and in the initial stages or in more serious cases, will usually apply these himself. While waiting for the vet to arrive it may be necessary to bandage the wound to stop bleeding. A good pad of cotton wool held firmly against the wound by a bandage (or by hand if the wound is in a position which cannot be bandaged) will usually stop bleeding, or at least slow it down sufficiently until help arrives. Tourniquets should not be used. If a flap of skin is present, the bandage should be put on so as to hold this in place. Applying a bandage will keep a wound clean until the vet arrives, when a decision can be made whether or not the wound needs stitching. Do not wash the wound with any disinfectant before the vet arrives. This may damage the tissues, which will prevent satisfactory healing if the wound has to be stitched. When dealing with wounds, a mild anti-bacterial disinfectant (one which does not damage tissues) should be used, not a strong one that is intended for disinfecting surfaces or buildings.

Injury or lameness in one limb will mean that extra weight will be placed on the opposite limb. Thus the "sound" limb should also be bandaged to provide support.

For reducing swelling from sprains, cold water hosing is beneficial – hosing for a quarter of an hour, two or three times a day, being sufficient. Re-freezable ice packs, that are held against the injured area by bandages, are also effective in reducing swelling but must be changed at frequent intervals.

If infection is present around a wound, application of heat will help to draw the poison.

With problems of the foot and lower limbs, such as swelling of the pastern, the horse can stand with the foot in a bucket of hot water ("hot tubbing"). For wounds higher up the leg, a hot "Animalintex" poultice can be applied.

In areas where it is impossible to use a bandage to keep a

poultice in place, such as on the back or jaw, heat can be applied by soaking a cloth or flannel in hot water, ringing it out, and holding it over the affected area (hot fomentation). If two cloths are used, one being soaked and one being applied to the skin, a continual application of heat can be maintained by alternating them.

Grooming. Cleanliness of the skin and coat is more necessary during sickness than at any other time. Grooming, besides achieving this, gives a better feeling of well-being and comfort and should not be omitted unless the nature of the case makes it impossible or undesirable. Remember to attend to the feet also. Perform these duties quickly, quietly and efficiently; this is no time for fussing and irritating the horse.

Administering Medicines. I have always stressed the similarity between horses and children, and never is this more noticeable than when medicines have to be given. "Gentleness and guile" is the motto when giving medicines to horses.

Powders, when thoroughly mixed with the favourite food are usually taken without any trouble, but horses have an acute sense of smell and easily detect any tampering with their food, so include some choice ingredient such as grated carrots well mixed in – or whatever is the particular fancy of your animal. A sprinkling of the same delicacy on top always proves tempting and lulls suspicion. Another solution is to put the powder between two pieces of bread – horses will often eat a medicated sandwich without fuss!

Nowadays, many wormers and some antibiotics come as a paste in a ready-loaded syringe. For a right-handed person it is easier to administer this form of treatment from the horse's right ("off") side. While someone else holds the horse on the near side by a head collar, stand on the right side and place the left hand on the bridge of the nose. The thumb can then be inserted into the space in the lip between the front teeth and cheek teeth, and pressed against the roof of the mouth which will make the horse open its mouth. The tip of the syringe is inserted to the back of the mouth, and its contents squeezed on to the tongue. The syringe is then quickly removed, and the horse's head is held in the air (by pressing under its jaw to keep its mouth shut) until it has swallowed. A syringe is an ideal way of giving cough medicines to horses.

It is not advisable to give liquid medicines to horses by "drenching" them. This is now an outdated procedure involving the use of a long-necked bottle or "drenching horn". There is considerable danger, when attempting to "drench" a sick or fractious horse, that some or all the liquid can enter its lungs, with serious consequences (pneumonia).

In the past, various cure-all remedies were used, particularly for colic. Most were fairly ineffective, and the volume given was usually far too small to make much impression on the voluminous contents of the equine bowels. In digestive disorders, such as colic, when liquids are needed, they are required in large volumes (two or more litres) which can only be safely administered by a vet using a stomach tube.

21

AILMENTS OF THE
LEG AND FOOT

LAMENESS

Seats of Lameness. The parts in which lameness most
commonly occurs are *below the knee or hock, particularly the
foot and the back tendons.* The knee itself, a complicated joint
with many small bones which distribute and minimise
concussion, suffers least. The shoulder, too, is comparatively
seldom affected, and when it is, the muscles are usually the seat
of injury by sprains or blows. Below the knee and hock there
are no muscles, and the tendons normally bear the strain – if
they do not the bone will fracture.

When the position of lameness cannot be immediately
located, the usual practice is to suspect the foot; the old saying
advises us to "remove the shoe, even if the horse is lame in the
head", and so many troubles originate in the foot that this is
sound advice. Here diagnosis is difficult, since the cause of the
trouble is completely hidden within the horny box of the hoof.

Which Leg? The question has caused a very great deal of head-
scratching and dispute, and many a sound leg has been long
and religiously treated by mistake. The following points are a
guide to solving the problem.

As indicated in "Attitude", page 165, standing in the stable
the horse may "point", or rest, a lame foreleg in front of the
other, while resting a hindleg is normal. Constant uneasiness
on one foot is also suspicious.

If such signs are absent, the horse should be taken out on to a
smooth, hard surface and "trotted up" – slowly away from,

and then back to, the examiner. It may be possible to gain a clue from any "favouring" of the affected limb and "dropping", or bearing more heavily, on the sound one. It is easiest to remember *"SINKS ON THE SOUND SIDE"*. He should be trotted up directly he is brought out of the stable, preferably after a rest, when stiffness is more pronounced.

Nodding the head at the trot is a reliable indication. When lame in front, it is dipped as the sound leg touches the ground, and raised on the lame one. Severe lameness in both forelegs often gives the impression of soundness, but, watching the action, "pottering" or stepping short, is noticeable. While determining the leg, in this way, it is often possible to find the position of the trouble. Turning the leg outwards indicates the knee or elbow, while dragging the toe, due to difficulty in forward movement of the leg, means the shoulder.

In a hind limb, lameness shows as uneven movement of the hindquarters when the horse is trotted away. The hind quarter on the corresponding side will be seen to rise when weight is put on the lame leg; the quarter on the opposite side will be seen to sink down when the sound leg hits the ground (again *"SINKS ON THE SOUND SIDE"*). However, if the horse is trotted back again it will be seen that the head nods slightly when the lame hind leg hits the ground. Thus there can be confusion between lameness in a hind limb and lameness in the diagonally opposite fore limb if the uneven movement of the hindquarters is not spotted. When "trotting up", it is also useful to look at the horse from the side to observe the arc of flight of the feet, the length of the stride and the way in which the feet are placed to the ground. Often, it can be noticed that one foot is not lifted as high off the ground, or takes a shorter stride than its opposite leg. One foot may land on the toe or land more heavily on the heel than normal (to save itself from bearing weight on a painful spot).

Finding the Position. The affected leg found, it should be felt for heat, tenderness or enlargements, and carefully compared with the sound one. If it appears normal, the next step is to have the shoe taken off and the foot searched for nails, bruises, corns, etc. Heat in the foot, or "pointing", usually means the trouble is in the foot, as does constantly lifting the foot – the latter indicating great pain.

The vet will usually examine the limbs in the same way but will check the joints by carefully flexing and extending each in turn. He may even hold a joint flexed for a period before trotting the horse up. This can make some joint problems, particularly spavin, show up better. He or she may also use hoof testers (special pincers) to apply pressure to various parts of the hoof to find a painful spot. If the site of lameness is still uncertain, one or more nerve blocks may be performed. By injecting local anaesthetic around the nerves at a certain level on the limb, the leg is temporarily desensitised below that point. Thus, if the seat of lameness is below the injection site, the pain will cease and the horse trots up sound. A nerve block at the pastern will make a horse with a foot problem go sound. If it is still lame, the problem is higher up the leg and further injections higher up will be needed to pin-point the trouble.

If bone damage or a problem within the foot is suspected, it may be considered necessary to take X-rays to assess the position and extent of the injury. Damaged muscle tissue causes changes in the blood which can easily be detected by blood tests. This can be useful for confirming or ruling out muscle injury as a possible cause of lameness – sometimes very helpful when dealing with back problems.

Causes of Lameness. Horses doing fast work on soft ground frequently suffer from strain of the tendons and ligaments, encouraged by bad riding, working when tired or on unsuitable "going".

Following long work on hard surfaces, particularly in draught horses, bony enlargements may appear, and it is while these are forming that lameness occurs. Sometimes, these bony enlargements occur in and around joints (as in articular ringbone and spavin) and interfere with their movement. A stilted action and sprain of the "check ligament", showing as a painful swelling immediately below the knee, are also liable to result from such work. The check ligament is the one which enables a horse to sleep standing, and is situated with the back tendons between the knee and fetlock.

Dislocations. When a joint is dislocated, the ligaments and muscles connected with it are usually sprained at the same time. Dislocations are, fortunately, extremely rare. Partial dislocations are sometimes seen in youngsters, at the fetlock or the patella (the "knee-cap" in the horse's stifle joint); this latter can often be heard to click back into place of its own accord. Complete dislocation is serious, but where muscles are more concerned than ligaments in holding the joint together, as in the shoulder, there is greater hope of full recovery.

The symptoms of dislocation are deformity, loss of use of the limb together with a shortening of it, and often painful swelling.

Dislocated bones can sometimes be returned to their normal position by manipulation, under general anaesthesia. In all cases of suspected dislocation, immediate veterinary attention is required.

Fractures. Fractures may be partial or complete, and are known as: simple, compound, comminuted, impacted, or greenstick.

Simple fractures are unaccompanied by external wounds, and the break may be across the bone (transverse), at an angle (oblique) or the full length of the bone (longitudinal).

Compound fractures show an external wound.

Comminuted fractures may be simple or compound, and the term means that the bone is broken into more than two portions – as in crushing.

Impacted fractures are those where the broken parts have been driven into each other.

Greenstick fractures are incomplete breaks, much in the manner that a green stick breaks. This kind is more common in young stock, whose bones are not so brittle as adults'.

Symptoms generally are pain and loss of function, followed by swelling. There is not the "fixing" of the parts which appears in a dislocation, and the broken parts can be heard grating on each other – "crepitation".

Treatment. If a fracture is suspected following a fall or some other accident, a vet should be called immediately to examine the animal on the spot – BEFORE it is moved. In many cases, simple fractures are turned into compound or comminuted ones by attempting to move an animal which has insufficient support for the damaged limb.

If an injured horse is down on the ground it may have difficulty in getting up, particularly if the damaged leg is underneath. It should be prevented from struggling and attempting to rise, by someone sitting or lying across the top of its neck to hold it down. A coat placed under its head may protect the lower eye from injury; a second coat over its eyes will calm it until help arrives. When sufficient help and ropes are available, it may be necessary to roll the horse over to help it get up.

Fractured limbs can be supported, to enable the horse to be moved, by applying thick layers of cotton wool, intertwined with bandages, to the leg and strengthening this arrangement with suitable material (e.g. a broom handle or a piece of plastic guttering).

Both splinting the leg and moving the horse should only be attempted under the supervision of a vet. Pain-killers will be needed and it may be necessary to sedate, or even anaesthetise, a horse to move it safely.

In the past, most horses with broken legs were destroyed to prevent suffering. This was because there was no satisfactory way of immobilising the leg to allow a fracture to heal. Continual movement as the horse struggled to get up and down also made matters worse; even putting the horse in slings did not restrict movement sufficiently to allow the bone to repair.

Today, orthopaedic plates and screws are available in sizes suitable for horses, and some limb fractures can be repaired in a similar manner to broken legs in humans. Also, the use of fibreglass to make casts, means that fractures in the lower part of the limb can now be effectively immobilised.

In practice, greenstick fractures usually heal well with rest and immobilisation. Some simple fractures of the lower parts of the limbs can be successfully treated by surgery and/or application of a fibre-glass cast. Comminuted fractures (with many small pieces) and fractures high up the leg are much graver propositions, and if it is considered that the fracture has no chance of healing, the horse may have to be destroyed.

The best course of action for any fracture can only be decided once the extent and position of the break is known.

This means that an X-ray is essential to assess the damage; only then can the most appropriate action be taken.

It should be noted that smaller fractures are often overlooked. Quite often, when X-rays are taken of a swollen joint, as part of a lameness examination, small fragments ("chips") of bone, which may be causing irritation, are found within the joint. Fractures of the splint bones are also often missed. What looks like a "splint" is, in fact, a fracture of this small bone which is easily brought about by a kick or knock. It may be necessary to remove the loosened end of the bone surgically to get a fractured splint bone to heal. Another frequently-overlooked fracture is a cracked rib (often resulting from a kick from another horse).

Arthritis (Degenerative Joint Disease). The activities we demand of our horses expose them to continual concussion. Although their feet and limbs have special structures to overcome this, wear and tear of the joints, as a result of concussion, is a common problem, particularly in old age. Arthritic changes are often encountered in the foreleg fetlock joints which become swollen as a result (causing articular "windgalls"). The pastern and coffin joints may also be affected – here the arthritis is known as articular ringbone – whilst in the hock, spavin is the result. Poor conformation, bad shoeing and over-use on hard surfaces all contribute to concussion which, over a long period, is likely to lead to trouble.

Horses with mild arthritis are usually stiff at first, but warm up. In more severe cases, the horse may be lame. Many of these animals have been treated with pain-killing anti-inflammatory drugs which enable them to remain "sound". However, in some cases, drugs such as butazolidin ("bute") take away the pain so effectively that horses that should be rested are worked, which can cause further damage to the joint. In other cases, old horses that are a bit stiff benefit from such treatment.

Recently, new drugs have been developed for treating degenerative joint diseases in horses. These can be injected directly into the affected joint to help the arthritic changes to heal. Also, by treating only the affected joint, rather than the whole horse, the problem of side-effects, which are sometimes encountered when anti-inflammatory drugs are given to horses by mouth, are overcome.

If a riding-horse tends to suffer from arthritis, regular exercise will often help (i.e. small amounts of work each day, rather than weekend riding).

Arthritis is very common in old horses. It is also usually worse in cold and wet weather. For this reason, it is often necessary to stable old horses during winter.

Sprains. The bones comprising joints are held together by ligaments, strong bands of tissue which protect them from over-extension. Muscles are attached to bones upon which they act, by tendons ("sinews"), almost inelastic cords which permit the full elasticity of muscles being used without injury.

When subjected to injury or excessive strain, from blows, sudden twists, concussion, etc., sprain of the ligaments or tendons results, accompanied by swelling, stiffness and tenderness.

Sprains are a common cause of lameness in the horse, and if they are not given sufficient time to heal, re-injury and further damage will make matters far worse. It sometimes happens that the bones themselves are injured or fractured in association with a sprain. This may sometimes only be revealed on an X-ray.

A vet should examine any horse with a sprain, particularly if it is severe. Sprains are not always immediately obvious. In many cases, little is seen at exercise and it is not until the evening that the heat, pain and swelling become obvious. This is why feeling the foreleg tendons (at the back of the cannon bones) usually forms part of the evening routine of horses doing hard work.

In every case immediate rest is essential. The object is to prevent any further damage or haemorrhage within the tendon. The next stage is to try and reduce the swelling. Cold-hosing, ice packs and physiotherapy equipment (ultra-sound or short-wave therapy) can all be used satisfactorily. The legs are bandaged to provide support (the opposite leg is also bandaged for support – as this will be required to take extra weight).

In severe sprains of the foreleg tendons, a shoe with a raised heel may be fitted to provide support and to ease tension on the damaged tendon. Alternatively, it may be necessary to fit a plaster cast to provide support, and to rest the leg.

The third stage in treatment is to promote healing. To try and achieve this, irritant lotions or pastes, known as "blisters", are sometimes applied to the skin over damaged tendons once the initial inflammatory reaction has "settled down". ("Blisters" attempt to increase the blood supply to the damaged area.) However, it is doubtful whether applying "blisters" to the skin has any effect on damaged tendons. It seems much more likely that any beneficial effect is due to the enforced rest which follows tendon treatment.

Various surgical operations have also been devised to try to improve and strengthen tendon healing. Whether or not any of these are advisable for a particular sprain should be discussed with the vet.

The rate of healing of any tissue depends on its blood supply. Muscles, well-supplied with blood vessels, heal quickly when injured. Tendons have a very poor blood supply, ligaments even worse, and healing in both is extremely slow. It takes at least six months for a damaged tendon to heal fully, probably even more. For a ligament, 9 months, at least, is needed. In most cases, time is the best healer – a spell at grass of 6–12 months for a tendon, and a minimum of 12 months for a serious ligament strain (such as a check ligament sprain).

FOOT PROBLEMS

In a healthy foot the wall is cool and sound, the sole hard but not brittle, and there is no offensive smell when normally clean.

The following are the commonest foot complaints and injuries, with notes on symptoms and treatment. Do not hesitate to seek professional advice when they are discovered.

Brittle Hoof. This is often a natural defect and is seen mostly in hot, dry weather. It makes shoeing difficult, as the hoof breaks away and gives little nail-hold, often leading to nails being driven too close to the sensitive structures and causing lameness. The application of oils to the crust (Neatsfoot Oil or Hoof Oil) increases the pliancy of the hoof, but repeated application of oil can prevent water being absorbed in the hoof and may actually contribute to its hardness. It may be better to

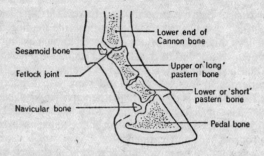

Fig. 15 The Bones of the Foot

"tub" the feet in warm water for five minutes daily for a few days, to soften the horn, before a good layer of oil is applied. This will then retain the water by preventing evaporation.

Brittle horn can be associated with nutritional deficiencies – particularly of biotin and calcium – and, in rare instances, zinc. Any horse that has poor quality horn, for any reason (especially as a result of laminitis), should be given a daily vitamin, mineral, and amino-acid supplement.

Canker. This is an infection of the horn of the sole. It was a common problem in carriage and draught horses in Victorian times. These were often kept in deplorable conditions, and the constant wetting of the sole by urine allowed infection to enter. Affected horses are not lame and the condition is easily cured by keeping the feet dry and treating the sole with astringent and antibiotic dressings. Improvements in stable management and hygiene mean that this condition is seldom seen nowadays.

Corns. These are bruises of the sensitive sole, at the angle of the heels, and may lead to abscesses. Concussion and pressure of the heel of the shoe, from faulty shoeing, are common causes, and flat and weak feet are most liable. The "economical" practice of keeping shoes on too long, so that the wall overlaps them, is a fruitful source of corns. The horse must be rested, without shoes; damaged horn should be removed and a poultice applied. When work is resumed it is advisable to use special shoes that relieve the sole of pressure.

Cracked Heels. This is a dermatitis of the heels and the back of the pasterns. It occurs as a result of irritation of the skin in this area by mud and wetting, which allows infection to enter. The skin surface cracks and oozes a serous discharge. The crack may heal but is opened again by movement of the pastern, and repeated cracking produces a raw, infected heel. The horse is usually lame and may snatch up the leg quickly in pain, holding it off the ground. Ointments are essential to promote healing and prevent cracking. Powders and antibiotic sprays, which tend to form scabs which crack again, should not be used. An antibiotic ointment should be applied to a dressing which is then placed against the raw area and held in place with a bandage. The horse must be rested until healing is complete, which may take some while. If infection is present and the leg becomes swollen, it may be necessary for the vet to give antibiotic injections. In horses that are prone to this problem, the use of a barrier cream (such as zinc oxide, zinc and castor oil, or Vaseline ointment) may protect the skin and prevent cracking. In most cases, the problem is caused by excessive wetting of the heels. For this reason, in winter, it is best to allow mud to dry and then brush it off later, rather than washing the heels with water.

Cracks in the Wall. These can be horizontal (a true sandcrack) or vertical (a false sandcrack). The former are uncommon, but can be caused by injury to the coronet. In practice, vertical cracks at the toe are commonly known as sandcracks, while those at the quarters are known as quarter cracks. Cracks running down from the coronet are more serious and are usually the result of injury to the coronary band. Cracks running up from the ground surface can be due to neglect (particularly in unshod horses at grass, whose feet are not trimmed) or to abnormal pressure on the hoof wall. The horse can be lame if the movement of the two sides pinches the sensitive tissues underneath. Also, infection may enter a deep crack, causing lameness when the sensitive layers below become infected.

Cracks tend to spread up the wall as a result of movement. If the crack can be immobilised it will "grow out", over a matter of months, as a result of new normal horn growing down from the coronary band to replace it. The farrier will usually cut a 'V' in the wall at the ground surface to relieve pressure on the base of the split. He will fit a shoe with a clip on either side of the crack to help prevent movement of the horn when the horse walks. A horizontal groove is then rasped at the apex of the crack to prevent it spreading upwards. Deeper cracks may require antibiotic treatment and may need to be immobilised by filling the crack with acrylic resin.

False Quarter. This is a defect in which a thin layer of brittle horn forms on the wall, and occurs mostly at the sides, where it is seen as a groove or series of grooves rather like Sandcracks. There is no lameness, but weakness of the heels of the foot. It arises from injury to the coronary band, often as a result of tread wounds. Special shoes may be needed to help provide additional support. Rarely, it may be necessary to strip away the hoof wall at this point in an attempt to stimulate growth of new healthy horn.

Forging. The common term for this, "Clicking", gives the clue to the trouble, striking a fore-shoe with a hind, usually at the trot. It seldom causes injury, although it may obviously be dangerous in some circumstances, but the continual click is annoying. Unschooled and unbalanced horses, particularly youngsters or those out of condition, are generally the culprits. A concave shoe may help in curing the noise. (See Chapter 15, pages 123 and 125.)

Laminitis or "Founder". This is a very painful inflammatory condition of the feet. Usually both forefeet are involved, but sometimes all four are affected. The animal is reluctant to get up or move and will stand with its hind legs well under it, trying to take as much weight on them as possible. If made to walk, it will be very "pottery" and will try to walk on its heels.

The pain arises from damage to the laminae at the front wall of the hoof, caused by alteration in blood flow within the feet. This is a result of toxins released elsewhere in the body – in most cases from the bowel, due to over-eating – but, less often, it can follow infection (e.g. pneumonia) elsewhere in the body.

Laminitis is most often seen in ponies. These cannot cope

with lush spring and summer grass or large amounts of concentrates. When such an animal has had laminitis once it is very likely to have it again in subsequent years. It can usually be prevented by putting the horse on sparse grazing at this time of year, but in some instances it may be necessary to remove the animal from grazing altogether and confine it to hay and water in a large yard.

Laminitis causes changes in the shape of the hoof. Long toes with rings in the walls ("laminitic rings") are caused by lack of wear and irregular horn growth. The attachment of the coffin (pedal) bone within the hoof to the hoof wall is loosened, such that it rotates downwards, pressing on the sole, causing a "dropped sole" which is flat, rather than the normal concave outline. The bone may even come through the sole, which may necessitate the animal's destruction on humanitarian grounds.

In laminitis, there is always heat in both forefeet and a bounding pulse can often be felt. A vet should be called immediately if laminitis is suspected, as the sooner pain-killers are given the better. This will enable the horse to walk, which helps relieve the blood congestion in the feet. It may be necessary to force the horse to walk, but improvement will soon follow if it does. Cold-hosing can also bring relief, but pain-killers and anti-inflammatory drugs will also be needed for several days.

Later, it may be necessary to attend to the hoof problems which are usually associated with chronic laminitis. This will involve both vet and farrier. The foot may need repeated trimming to restore a normal-shaped hoof, and special shoes may be needed. Horses and ponies that have had laminitis tend to be "footy", having a dropped sole which is more sensitive to ground pressure. For this reason, such animals usually benefit from having shoes on all the time, even when at grass. Feed supplements should be given to promote healthy horn growth. (See "Brittle Hoof", page 181.)

Navicular Disease. This condition, which usually affects middle-aged horses (it is very rare in ponies), is caused by degenerative changes in the small navicular bone which lies inside a horse's hoof just above the point of the frog. Both forelegs are usually affected, though at first, lameness may be more obvious in one leg. At the outset the lameness may be intermittent, but tends to be progressive, leading to permanent lameness. The horse often has a "pottery" gait – because it is lame in both forelegs – and tries to land its foot on the toe to avoid pressure on the heels where the navicular bone lies. This causes excess wear of the front shoes at the toe and may cause the horse to stumble.

For many years, the disease was incurable, often resulting in the horse being destroyed on humanitarian grounds. Research has shown that the degenerative changes in the bone are due to changes in its blood supply. There is still argument about the cause of these changes, but treatment with anticoagulants and drugs, to improve the foot circulation, are now being used for this condition. These can produce a cure in about 60% of cases. It seems likely that this long-toe/low-heel foot conformation fault can be a contributing factor to this problem. Owners should ensure that this is put right by their farrier. (See "Balancing" the foot, page 119.)

Over-Reach. The upper part of the forefoot, at the heels or higher, is often cut by the toe of the hind at the gallop; an uncollected horse is always liable to over-reach, or it may be caused by weakness, when jumping, or pulling up sharply. The injury requires wound treatment, washing with cold water and dressing antiseptically, and endeavours must be made to prevent its recurrence. (See also Chapter 15, "Clips", page 123.)

Pricks. There are two ways in which a foot may be pricked: (1) in shoeing, (2) by picking up a nail or similar object. The first will usually be evident at the time and is the farrier's responsibility. In either case, the shoe must be removed as soon as possible and the foot poulticed every four hours to draw out the poison. Nails embedded deeply into the foot may damage or allow infection to enter important structures deep within it, with serious consequences. Nails penetrating deeply into the frog are the worst offenders, as they may affect the tendon beneath it.

Tetanus can result from pricks and puncture wounds to the foot. It is essential, if the horse is not vaccinated against tetanus, that it should receive protection against this disease by being given an injection of tetanus anti-toxin soon after the injury. In deep puncture wounds of the foot, the vet should always be called in to examine and treat the foot. Antibiotic injections are often necessary to prevent infection.

Pus in the Foot. This is one of the commonest causes of lameness. Infection can enter the sole through small cracks or as a result of penetration by a sharp object, such as a small stone (usually a flint) or a nail. The pus which results causes extreme pain by pressing on the sensitive layers beneath the sole. There is heat in one foot only, and the horse is reluctant to put weight on it.

The vet may be able to detect where the pus lies by applying pressure to the sole with hoof testing pincers. He can then cut down through the horn of the sole to release the trapped pus. The foot is then poulticed for one or more days to draw out any remaining poison.

It is often not obvious where the pus lies. In this case, the shoe must be removed and the foot poulticed for one or more days to soften the horn and draw the pus to a head.

A plug of cotton wool is inserted into the hole, to prevent mud entering, until it is closed by new horn growth. If a large hole has to be made, it may be kept clean by inserting a piece of leather across the sole, under the shoe when it is refitted.

Quittor. This is a chronic discharge of pus from a hole in the skin (sinus) at the coronet. It occurs when the lateral cartilage of the pedal bone becomes infected as a result of a deep wound at the coronet. This was a common problem in driving-horses, resulting from tread wounds, but is seldom seen in riding-horses. Treatment usually involves an operation to open the sinus and remove the infected portion of cartilage, after which the problem usually clears up quickly.

Ringbone. This is a horseman's term for new bone being formed around the pastern or pedal bones. It is sometimes called high ringbone when it is around the pastern joint and bones, and low ringbone when around or near the coffin (pedal) joint. Often the new bone is formed inside the joint (articular ringbone) which is more serious as it interferes with joint movement. This is, in fact, arthritis, resulting from degeneration of the joint cartilage (degenerative joint disease). In some cases, new bone may be a result of damage to the bone from a blow, or due to sprain of a ligament where it attaches to the bone. If this is not near a joint this form of ringbone may "settle down" with rest and the horse may become sound. A hard swelling at the front of the leg just above the coronet is suspicious of ringbone. X-rays are usually required to decide what treatment is necessary. Although anti-inflammatory drugs may help in mild cases, ringbone involving joints is serious and frequently puts an end to the animal's working life.

Sandcrack. (See "Cracks in the Wall", page 183.)

Seedy Toe. In Seedy Toe, the white line is injured by inflammation, affecting the secretion of horn and causing separation between the hoof casing and the horny laminae, starting at the toe. Laminitis is generally to blame, but it occasionally arises from weakness or from pressure by the shoe clip. It is noticeable, when the shoe is removed, by the absence of the white line in places, or the hollowness can be detected by tapping the wall. The cavity exposed, on removal of the shoe, must be probed and cleaned. Part of the wall may have to be rasped away to remove mealy horn, and the hole can be packed with cotton wool swabs to prevent dirt entering; this will allow the seedy toe to "grow out" with new horn growth. Lameness does not usually occur unless infection enters deeply into the horn.

Sidebones. This is a horsekeeper's term for hardening of the lateral cartilages attached to the pedal bone inside a horse's hoof. These cartilages actually become bone, and this is a normal occurrence in all horses in old age. In some horses, this ossification can occur when they are young, and very rarely is associated with lameness. The hardness or otherwise of the cartilages can be felt just above the coronet above the quarters of the hoof. In the past, sidebones were frequently thought to be a cause of lameness, when the trouble was actually elsewhere.

Thrush. This is the term used when the horn of the frog becomes infected and rotten. It becomes black, with a characteristic cheesy smell that cannot be mistaken. It is usually caused by failure to pick out the feet properly. Mud and droppings packed into the frog clefts allow moisture to be absorbed into the frog, softening it. This allows bacteria, which are present in soil and droppings, to enter the horn (which they are not able to do unless it is softened) and set up infection. Horses with "boxy", upright feet and small frogs have more space for material to be trapped in, and may be more prone to thrush.

Thrush is normally a problem in stabled horses but can occur in winter, at grass, as a result of continual wetting. Lameness does not occur except when infection enters deeper into sensitive tissues below the frog. The frog must be cleaned and all rotten horn removed. The frog and its clefts can then be treated daily with an astringent, such as 10% formalin, copper sulphate solution, or tincture of iodine. Aerosols containing antibiotics and gentian violet (blue sprays) are ideal for thrush. Clean bedding and good foot care should prevent this problem. Some horses are particularly prone to thrush, and for this reason are unsuited to deep litter bedding or wintering out.

Treads. These are similar wounds to Over-Reaches but are inflicted on the hindfeet by the front toe of another horse. Because of the danger of this, riders should always keep a full horse-length behind the animal in front when going in single file. Treatment is the same as for Over-Reaches.

THE PASTERN AND FETLOCK

Brushing. This defective action, in either the fore or hindlegs, is striking or brushing the lower part of one leg – usually at the fetlock or the coronet – with the opposite foot. Although at most times trifling, it may cause swelling of the affected part, and lameness. Bad conformation, tiredness, poor condition and faulty shoeing are all causes. When due to the first, the only prevention is the use of a "Brushing" or "Yorkshire Boot", of felt or rubber, fitting over the fetlock joint, or an exercise bandage as a substitute. (See also "Speedy Cutting", page 191.)

Fractures. (See page 177.)

Ringbone. (See page 187.)

Sesamoiditis. The term means inflammation of the small Sesamoid Bones situated behind the fetlock. It arises from injury either to the bones or their ligaments or tendons, setting up inflammation. There is swelling and tenderness of the joint, which appears to be displaced forwards, and the lameness causes short-stepping. In the early stages, the inflammation can be reduced by rest and cold water. Support should be given by a loose, thick layer of cotton wool securely held by a bandage of some firm material, such as calico; the trouble must not be aggravated by pressure, and the bandage should be removed and renewed daily.

Fracture of the Sesamoid Bones may sometimes occur as a result of severe injury. This can be detected by X-ray examinations of the fetlock. In all cases of damage to the Sesamoid Bones (and the suspensory ligament which is attached to them), a long period of rest (at least six months, but preferably 12 months) will be necessary.

THE FORELEG: BELOW THE KNEE

Sprain of the Flexor (Back) Tendons. All horses are liable to sprain of these tendons from an unlucky twist or from concussion when jumping. Frequent resting of the leg and stepping short are the first signs, followed by swelling. After sprain treatment (page 180), a long rest at grass is advised.

Breakdown. This term includes any fractures or sprains which permit the fetlock to drop, sometimes as far as the ground. It occurs most commonly in horses of speed, and spells finish to their career on the course or in the hunting field. When only slight, eventual recovery may take place, but only slow work will be possible. Long, professional treatment is required, and while waiting for attention, the hollow of the heel should be packed with any soft material at hand and bandaged in position. Cold water will help to reduce inflammation, and after recovery there should be a long rest at grass.

Speedy Cutting. This is similar to Brushing, but the injury is inflicted higher on the leg, often on the inside of the knee. Cause and treatment are as for Brushing. (See also page 69.)

Splint. A bony exostosis, or extra growth, joining the Splint Bone to the Cannon, is liable to follow inflammation to the covering membrane (Periosteum), caused by direct injury or concussion. Splints are more often seen in young horses, as a result of over-work on hard going. The enlargement is found usually on the inner side of the foreleg, either immediately under the knee – where it may "creep" and interfere with that joint – or anywhere beween there and where the Splint Bone ends. It does occasionally form on the outside of the foreleg and even on the hind. Lameness is present in the early stages while the growth is developing but generally disappears when the two bones have finally joined. Many horses over five or six years old have splints which no longer cause trouble and are passed over as of no consequence. When the Splint cannot be seen or felt, it can be detected by the extreme tenderness of the affected part. Lameness shows best at the trot on hard ground.

Rest is necessary while the Splint is active, and anti-inflammatory drugs can be painted over the area which, when absorbed, reduce the reaction. At a later stage, applying a mildly irritant lotion or paste ("blister") over the Splint may be helpful in reducing the swelling. The possibility of a fracture of the Splint Bone should not be overlooked. (See "Fractures", page 177.)

Windgalls. Small, soft swellings are often found around the fetlocks in the forelegs. Similar swellings are also sometimes

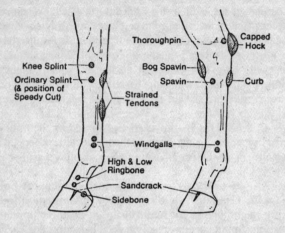

Fig. 16 Ailments found in the lower Fore- and Hind Leg

seen in the hind limbs. These swellings were once thought to contain air (hence the name) but are, in fact, accumulations of joint or tendon fluid. Most often, the swelling occurs towards the back of the fetlock, either side of the flexor tendons. This is a swelling in the tendon sheath (tendinous windgall). It is usually a result of hard work, especially on hard ground. It will not cause lameness, but may remain as a permanent blemish. A period of rest and a supporting bandage, applied when the swelling first occurs, may prevent it becoming permanent.

Less often, a soft, fluid-filled swelling is seen on either side of the leg just behind the cannon bone. This is a swelling of the fetlock joint (articular windgall) resulting from strain of the joint or arthritis. Lameness is often present and veterinary advice should be sought. A swelling at this site is more serious than a tendinous windgall, which is of little significance.

THE FORELEG: THE KNEE AND ABOVE

Broken Knees. Broken knees are nearly always the result of a fall, and include – besides fractures of the bones – bruises and open wounds. It is possible that there may be penetration of a tendon sheath or of the knee joint itself, so that it as well to have the wound examined by an expert. Absolute cleanliness is essential, and to make removal of dirt easier, the leg should be bent during cleansing. Antiseptic dressings should be used, and inflammation reduced with cold water. The wound will have to be bandaged and dressed for 1–2 weeks to keep it clean, and antibiotics may be necessary to control infection.

Hygroma of the Knee. Sometimes a large swelling occurs over the knee after a fall or, more often, after hitting a jump. The swelling is soft, fluid-filled, usually painless and does not cause lameness. The swelling can be caused by excessive accumulation of fluid in a tendon sheath, as a result of the injury, or by rupture of a large blood vessel that crosses the knee. Cold-hosing, ice packs and bandages may reduce the swelling if it is small. Sometimes it may be necessary to open and drain larger ones. Re-injury can make the problem much worse. Plenty of bedding and a rest from jumping are needed.

Capped Elbow. The commonest cause of capped elbow, indicated by swelling, is long contact with hard surfaces – a bare patch of floor in the stable, or the shoe, when lying down. The swelling can be dispersed by hot or cold fomentations twice a day, and precautions must be taken against recurrence. If insufficient bedding is not to blame, inspect the shoeing to see if the heels are too long. A method of prevention is an "elbow protector" or "preventer" also known as a "sausage boot"; this is a semi-circular bolster-like pad easily made from materials at hand, or which can be bought from a saddler. It fits around the *pastern.*

Elbow Lameness. This may result from sprain, fracture or arthritis, and is shown by standing with the leg bent. Treatment must be directed to the particular cause.

Fractures. In the forearm there is the main bone, the Radius, with a smaller bone behind, the Ulna, which can be felt as a projection at the elbow. When one of these is fractured, the other may help as a natural splint, but the injury is serious. The usual signs of a break can be detected either at the front of the arm or at the back, according to the bone affected. When applying splints, see that they are continued below the knee to prevent its movement.

Shoulder Lameness. Shoulder lameness may be brought on by injury, sprain or arthritis. Symptoms are stiffness, dragging the toe, and an outward movement of the leg. They must be considered in conjunction with known facts, and professional advice should always be sought. Injuries and sprains should have the usual cold water treatment, with a long rest.

Fractures. (1) Humerus, or Arm Bone. This bone extends from the elbow to the Scapula, or Shoulder Blade, with which it forms the "Point of Shoulder". Fracture is rare, but usually means the end of the horse's working life and, frequently, destruction on humanitarian grounds.

(2) Scapula (Shoulder Blade). This fracture can be detected by crepitation. The mass of muscle here is a protection, and keeps the broken parts in position when there is a fracture. Although small simple fractures can sometimes heal with rest, comminuted fractures (many pieces) usually necessitate destruction of the animal.

THE HINDLEG

Lymphangitis. The sufferers are usually hard-worked horses that have been rested for one or more days on a full working ration. Usually one hindleg, but rarely a foreleg, becomes very swollen. There is acute lameness. The limb is tender and painful and becomes enormous, the swelling often extending up to the groin. The horse usually has a fever and is very dull and "sorry for itself". Serum may ooze from the affected leg.

Treatment involves injections of antibiotics, diuretics, and anti-inflammatory and pain-killing drugs. Walking exercise, several times a day, helps restore the circulation and disperse the swelling. This problem is prevented by cutting back the concentrate ration and, if possible, turning a horse out on days when it is not doing any work. It is one of the reasons why horses' rations must always be adjusted daily according to their work.

THE HOCK

Capped Hock. This is a soft swelling on the point of the hock. It is caused by injury: through kicking the stable walls; from a blow when travelling in a trailer or horsebox; or when getting up and down on a hard floor with insufficient bedding. Hock Boots (see "Clothing", page 68) can be worn for protection when travelling, or if the horse kicks in the box, padding the walls may also help.

Kaolin poultices are usually sufficient to reduce the swelling. Lameness does not occur, but the swelling can be an ugly blemish. Sometimes it is necessary to drain fluid to get the swelling to go. Veterinary advice should always be sought about the most suitable treatment.

Curb. Curb is an enlargement at the back of the hock, due to sprain of tendons or ligaments from over-exertion, in jumping or galloping in deep, holding ground, and is found particularly in young horses. Excessively angled hocks ("sickle hocks"), predisposed to this problem, are sometimes called "curby hocks". The swelling, which is usually hard, appears a hand's breadth below the point of the hock, and both legs are usually affected. Slight lameness may be seen but this does not always occur. The swelling will usually settle down and disappear with rest and local anti-inflammatory treatment. Sometimes a mildly irritant lotion (known as a working "blister") is used later on to help reduce the swelling. If the horse is not rested a permanent blemish may result but this does not cause any problem other than an unsightly appearance.

Spavin. (Bone Spavin or Jack Spavin). This is a hard, bony swelling on the lower aspect of the inside of the hock joint. Both legs are usually affected. Lameness may only be seen in one leg, and it is not until a nerve block is performed that lesser lameness in the opposite leg is noticed. The swelling is due to new bone formation around the joints between the smaller bones at the base of the hock. Lameness is seen initially but in time the bones of the joint may fuse together and pain ceases, the horse remaining sound. Spavin is more common in horses with poor hind leg conformation, such as "cow hocks". Affected animals take shortened strides with their hind legs, which are not lifted high enough off the ground (lowered arc of flight), and there is excessive wear of the toes of the hind shoes. Anti-inflammatory drugs and rest may help the problem to settle down. Rolled toes and raised heels on the hind shoes may also be beneficial. Sometimes the horse may remain permanently lame and it may be advisable to perform surgery to improve the situation.

Cleveland Bay

Bog Spavin. This is a soft swelling of the hock joint itself. It is caused by over-working, particularly in young horses with weak hind legs. Lameness is rare. The problem usually settles down with rest. In some cases the swelling persists for a long time and it may be necessary for the vet to drain the excess fluid from the joint.

Sprained, or "Sprung" Hock. The Hock is often sprained in fast work, jumping or in heavy draught work. In minor cases only the ligaments are affected, but in others the bones and tendons may also be involved, and a sprung hock must always be regarded as requiring veterinary assistance. There is great pain, with tenderness and heat, and perhaps a high degree of fever. Prolonged, complete rest is necessary, with cold water treatment.

Thoroughpin. This is a fluid distension on either side of the Achilles tendon, just above the point of the hock, which can be pressed through to the other side by the finger – hence the old name, "Through-pin". Strain of some kind is the usual cause, but there is generally hereditary predisposition. Unless severe, the condition is not serious and there may be little or no lameness; it can be compared with Windgalls. With rest and massage the fluid will probably disperse, but sometimes it is drawn off surgically. High-heeled shoes can bring relief, as can rest and the local application of anti-inflammatory drugs.

ABOVE THE HOCK

Stifle Lameness. Lameness in the stifle may be due to sprain, bruise of the joint, or, generally, dislocation of the patella, or knee-cap. The common causes are falling, twisting, strain when starting with a heavy load in draught horses, or stable accidents such as slipping, getting cast, turning in a narrow space and striking the joint against door jambs, etc.

Young horses, particularly those with very straight hind legs are prone to dislocation (upward fixation) of the patella (knee cap). This causes the stifle to "lock" so that the leg is held straight out behind the horse, which drags the toe as it walks. The displaced patella can be seen as an enlargement on the outer surface of the stifle. Often, this unlocks itself spontaneously, accompanied by a sharp click. Making the horse walk backwards will usually free the knee-cap. If this problem occurs in older horses, it may be necessary to perform an operation to cut a small ligament to prevent it happening. Most young horses will grow out of it.

Hip Joint. Sprain and injury cause lameness in this joint from similar causes as in stifle lameness. It may also be due to arthritis. There is difficulty in moving the leg, which appears shorter and is swung outwards with dragging of the toe; pain is severe and there is considerable heat and tenderness. Hip problems are always serious and seldom come right, even with a long rest.

BACK AND PELVIS

A number of conditions in these regions of the horse's body can cause lameness, but more often produce stiffness, loss of action, or reluctance to jump.

Azoturia. ("Monday Morning Disease", or "Setfast"). This is a muscle problem, mainly affecting the hindquarter muscles which become very hard and painful. This problem occurs during exercise on the day after the horse has had a rest but has still been given a full working ration – as often happened in carthorses rested over the weekend, hence "Monday Morning Disease". The pain is often extreme, and moving the horse causes further muscle damage. The vet should be called out to examine the horse where it is; no attempt should be made to move it until it has been treated.

The muscle damage causes dark, discoloured, strong-smelling urine (hence azoturia) to be passed. Rest, pain-killers and careful attention to the diet are needed. The problem can be prevented by feeding according to work. Some horses are prone to this problem, and regular exercise, and a long period of slow work to warm up, is helpful in preventing trouble. Mild forms of this condition can cause loss of performance. Luckily, damaged muscle can be detected by blood tests, so that this is one cause of trouble that can be easily ruled out, or confirmed, by a blood test. The same test is useful to judge the extent of the damage, when it has settled down, so that the horse can begin work again safely.

Injuries to the Pelvis. The point of the hip is often knocked off by young horses rushing through a doorway. These may be sore for a few days but do not cause permanent problems. Occasionally, fractures of the pelvis occur as a result of a fall. These often heal well if the horse is rested, that is, unless the fracture involves the hip, when the outlook is usually hopeless. Mares that have had a previous fractured pelvis may have difficulty at foaling.

Back Problems. Injuries to back muscles and sprain of ligaments in the back occur as a result of jarring or accidents (such as getting cast in the box). The horse loses its suppleness, fails to use itself properly and may be reluctant to jump. Sometimes a painful area can be found but often it is difficult to pin-point the exact source of the trouble. Rest and anti-inflammatory drugs usually relieve the symptoms.

22

COMMON AILMENTS
AND INJURIES

NOTIFIABLE DISEASES

There are certain "scheduled diseases" which the law requires to be notified to the police, the local authority or the Ministry of Agriculture's veterinary inspector. Although not common, they should be mentioned. These are: Anthrax; Parasitic Mange (see page 204); Glanders or Farcy; Epizootic Lymph-angitis and Rabies. The last three no longer occur in the U.K., and the first two are extremely rare in horses.

POISONING

Poisoning in horses is also rare, and when it does occur is usually from vegetable origin. Horses are less likely than other animals to eat poisonous plants, and whilst most cases can be traced to garden cuttings, nothing should be left to chance.

Owners should thoroughly inspect new pasture, particularly hedges, and periodic checks should be carried out. Greediness for green food when first turned out, or during a dry summer, may lead to the animal exercising less than normal "choosiness" when grazing.

Hedge clippings represent the biggest threat, as horses will often eat these, whereas they are much less likely to eat the growing plant. The unexplainable human penchant for dumping hedge clippings in someone else's field poses a constant threat.

Ragwort is a common weed in horse pastures which can cause liver damage and nervous signs if eaten. Horses do not usually eat it unless it has been cut and wilted (hence the danger of Ragwort in hay) or there is little else to eat. This plant should be cut or weed-killed, removed and burnt. Horse-tails (Equisetum), another paddock weed, can be poisonous but is not often eaten unless it has been cut.

Many agricultural chemicals, in common use as herbicides and pesticides, are potentially extremely toxic to animals. Avoid grazing recently-treated pasture, and contact with contaminated water and containers used for these products.

Dangerous Plants include: Aconites (Monkshood); Boxwood; Bracken; Cow-bane; Darnel (seeds); Deadly and Woody Nightshade; Foxgloves; Hellebore; Hemlock; Henbane; Horse-tails (Equisetum); Laburnum; Laurel; Lupins; Meadow Saffron (Autumn Crocus); Oak (leaves and acorns); Privet; Ragwort; Rhododendron; and Yew.

Yew contains a very deadly poison. Although some horses have grazed near Yew trees for many years and left them alone, Yew can kill a horse in five to ten minutes, so it is safest for horses to avoid any grazing near this.

It is worth mentioning, however, that I have had horses which, although well-fed, showed a great liking for Privet and Laurel, eating large quantities without ill-effects.

Symptoms. Except in the case of Meadow Saffron, Bracken and Ragwort, the symptoms of poisoning show quickly. The commonest are; purging, excessive flow of saliva, dryness of the mouth, distension of the stomach, colic pains, feverish conditions, giddiness, dilated pupils, convulsions, stupor, paralysis, or loss of consciousness.

Treatment. Put the animal in a comfortable loose-box and send for professional assistance *immediately*, giving all relevant facts at the time, including, if possible, the nature of the poison. While waiting, the layman can take certain emergency measures. Any of the following will help:-

1. Frequent doses (284 ml, or ½ pint) of strong black *boiled* coffee or tea, particularly if Yew poisoning is suspected. If possible, this should be given using a syringe (an old worming syringe will do) rather than attempting to

"drench" the horse (see "Administering Medicines", page 172).

2. Encourage the horse to drink plenty of water; salt may be added to the food or water for this purpose.

3. If chemical poisoning is suspected, the source should, if possible, be identified accurately to assist treatment.

WOUNDS AND INJURIES

Abscess. This is a swelling containing pus, caused by germs. For safety, the vet should be asked to give an anti-tetanus injection; he will probably also supply a tube of penicillin for daily injections into the wound. The abscess should be fomented continually to bring it to a pointed, soft "head", when it can be lanced, and subsequently dressed as a wound. (See also "Strangles", page 209.)

Galls. (1) Girth. Girth galls take the form of either swellings or soreness. The first is from tight girthing, the second from loose girthing, soft condition, or a hard girth. Swellings should be massaged, and rubs treated as ordinary wounds; in neither case should the horse be saddled again until the skin is normal. A useful dressing is a lotion made of Lead Acetate and Zinc Sulphate; 2 teaspoons of each dissolved in a third of a litre (1½ pints) of water.

But prevention must be the aim. Some horses, owing to shape, gall easily; for these, a safeguard is a girth sleeve made of sheepskin or suitable synthetic material, which is placed around the girth at the part rubbed. If the saddle continually slides forward, a crupper may help, that is, a strap buckled to the cantle and forming a loop for the tail. As most horses "blow themselves out" during girthing, the girth should be tightened soon after mounting. It should also be re-checked when exercise lasts for more than two hours, when it may also need adjusting.

(2) Saddle. Saddle galls also appear as either swellings or abrasions, from pressure or rubbing. Causes are badly-fitting saddles, slack girthing, and loose, unbalanced riding. The saddle must stay in the tack room until the back is cleared and then there must be no reason for recurrence. In the meantime,

wound treatment can be given to abrasions (Gall Lotion), and swellings bathed with salt and water – one teaspoonful to half a litre (1 pint).

Some thin-skinned animals are particularly prone to pressure sores. In this case, the skin of the withers and back in contact with the saddle can be thickened by dabbing on Witch Hazel or Surgical Spirit daily. Neither of these should be applied if a pressure sore is already present as they will sting and cause irritation.

Mouth Injuries. These are usually found on the tongue, the corners of the lips, or the gum, and are caused by "ham-fisted" handling, badly-fitting bits, etc., and occasionally by sharp objects taken in with the food, a twig of hawthorn in the hay, for example. The essential part of the treatment is to hang up the bridle until the injury is *completely* healed – then be sure faults are corrected. When the tongue is cut, the mouth should be washed out after feeding, and boracic lotion will help. When eating is painful, soft food, such as bran, must be fed while the mouth is tender.

Wounds. For all wounds, however slight, it is wise to have a vet give an anti-tetanus injection as soon as possible. However, since tetanus can occur as a result of the smallest wound, it is preferable to have the horse permanently vaccinated against the disease, thereby avoiding the trouble and expense of giving tetanus antitoxin every time a wound, no matter how slight, occurs.

In serious cases the first consideration is to stop bleeding, by pressure bandaging above, below and directly over the wound. Then professional help must be obtained – stitching may be necessary.

In minor wounds, cleanliness is of greatest importance. A solution of mild antiseptic, such as Savlon, not strong disinfectant, should be used to wash and clean such a wound. This must obviously be diluted strictly according to the manufacturers' instructions. If this is not available, salt water can be used (one teaspoon of salt to half a litre (1 pint) of water). For puncture wounds, or very contaminated wounds, a solution of hydrogen peroxide is a useful and effective cleaning agent. Bandages will usually be applied to keep the wound clean and to prevent the formation of "proud flesh" (see page 171). Antibiotic ointment will prevent infection and will also stop the dressing of cotton wool or gamgee tissue sticking to the wound. Very small wounds can be left exposed to the air, which speeds up scab formation and healing. Undue wetting of wounds should be avoided, as this stimulates "proud flesh". Dabbing with moist cotton wool is usually sufficient to keep a wound clean.

AILMENTS WITH SKIN AND COAT SYMPTOMS

Lice. Two types are found on horses – biting and sucking lice, the latter usually infesting the roots of long hair, such as the mane and tail. Both are common in winter, and especially in early spring. Extreme irritation results, and rubbing causes hair loss from head and neck, and raw areas from self-inflicted injury. Blood loss through heavy infestation with sucking lice can make the animal anaemic, and weight loss may occur.

Affected horses can be treated with an anti-parasitic wash or dusted with louse powder at weekly intervals. Lice are becoming so common that it is advisable to dust horses with louse powder once a week as a preventive measure at this time of year. Lice lay eggs on the horse, not in the buildings or bedding. These eggs are resistant to parasiticides which are, however, capable of killing newly hatched lice (nits). Thorough grooming is the way to remove lice eggs from the coat. The adult insects can live for short periods off the horse and may be inadvertently transmitted to other horses using the same stable, tack, rug or grooming kit. If a horse has had lice, everything with which it has been in contact (particularly the woodwork of the buildings and its grooming kit) should be given a thorough clean with an insecticidal wash. Horse lice cannot live on man; the fleas of other domestic animals and the lice of humans are not found on the horse.

Mange. (See also page 200.) For practical purposes, these diseases are very unlikely to be encountered, but horsekeepers should be aware of their existence, which can be in two forms – dry and moist. Although there are exceptions, all cases should be regarded as highly contagious to other animals, *including man*, and skilled attention must be obtained. Under the Parasitic Mange Order the disease must be notified to the police. Almost any part of the horse may be affected, including the inside of the ears.

In the dry form the parasites burrow beneath the skin, but affect only the surface in the moist.

The symptoms are severe irritation, shedding of the hair in patches, the formation of small pimples, scabs or ulcers, or hardening and furrowing of the skin. In serious cases there is rapid falling away in conditon, followed by death.

The owner's part in treatment must be to prevent the disease spreading – by strict isolation and thorough disinfection.

Mud Fever. This is caused by the same organism as Rainscald, but here the problem occurs on the legs as a result of constant wetting by mud. It is seen on the skin over the cannon bones, particularly on the front of the hind legs, just below the hocks. Treatment is as for Rainscald, except that swelling of the legs sometimes makes it necessary to give antibiotic injections. Both conditions can be prevented by providing shelter in a paddock and brushing the dried mud from the legs in winter. Some horses may need to be stabled at this time of year to prevent the problem.

Rainscald. This is a bacterial skin infection which is seen in winter on the backs of horses that live out. The condition arises when matted coats are constantly wetted. Small matts of hair with pus beneath them are seen on the back and, especially, on the hindquarters. The disease is treated by washing off the scabs, using an anti-bacterial wash. Once these are removed, the infection usually clears up. A solution of 1% Potash Alum can be dabbed on to the raw area beneath the scab to aid healing.

Ringworm. This is a highly contagious disease in which a fungus grows at the roots of the hair, which becomes matted and falls out to disclose scurfy patches of skin covered with grey scales. These areas gradually increase in size and merge into other patches. Bad management, dirty conditions, etc., are the usual causes.

In treatment, remember the disease is contagious to humans as well as other animals, therefore isolation and disinfection are necessary. Tack, grooming kit and rugs are the usual means of spread, though direct contact from infected horses also occurs. For this reason, each horse should have its own tack, rugs and grooming equipment which are not used on others. Many disinfectants do not kill the Ringworm spores, which can remain on these articles for long periods and may infect other horses. It is best to ask your vet to recommend a disinfectant that *does* kill these spores.

There are many fungicidal medications with which Ringworm can be effectively treated by application to the affected areas. If the horse is covered with spots it may be preferable to give a suitable fungicide (Griseofulvin) by mouth, rather than treating each spot individually. Horses with Ringworm should not be groomed, as this tends to spread the disease.

Skin Growths. Horses quite often suffer from Skin Growths. The commonest are the wart-like sarcoids which are often found on the belly and in the groin. These can bleed or get in the way of tack and may have to be removed surgically. Rarely, Skin Growths can be cancerous. It is best to ask your vet to examine any Skin Growths on your horse, especially if they are growing rapidly.

Sweet Itch. This is another condition which causes itching but it only occurs during summer. This problem only affects a few individual horses (about 1.5% of the horse population) which are allergic to the saliva of certain biting midges (Culicoides pulicaris) which are active around dusk in the summer months. Affected animals rub the mane and tail causing extensive self-inflicted injury. This can be treated with soothing lotions, and the irritation reduced by anti-inflammatory drugs.

Affected animals suffer this problem each year and it can be prevented by stringent measures designed to stop the horse being bitten by midges. These include stabling the animal from 4.00 pm onwards in stables with fly-proof mesh grilles on doors and windows, and vigorous application of fly repellants and sprays to the horse and its stable. In spite of these measures the problem can still occur, as it may only take one midge bite to start a reaction. Wherever possible, it is best to avoid buying a horse that suffers from Sweet Itch.

Urticaria. (Sometimes called "Nettlerash".) This is seen as large, fluid-filled weals in the skin. These appear suddenly all over the body and are due to an allergy to something with which the horse has come into contact – either that it has eaten or something in its surroundings, such as bedding materials or pasture plants. In most cases it disappears in a few hours without treatment. Occasionally, a similar skin appearance may follow after a horse has rolled in nettles – hence the confusion over names!

AILMENTS WITH RESPIRATORY SYMPTOMS

In infectious respiratory conditions, nursing, strict isolation and disinfection are important. As a further precaution against spread of infection, isolation of affected animals should be attempted wherever possible.

Chronic Obstructive Pulmonary Disease (COPD). This very common cause of ill-health, which used to be known as "Broken Wind", is a man-made problem produced by keeping horses in a stable environment contaminated with fungal spores. It does not occur in horses in the wild or in domestic horses at grass. It is due to an allergy to mould spores in the dust released from fodder and bedding. The importance of adequate ventilation and spore-free fodder and bedding, in preventing this problem, have been discussed in previous chapters (see pages 30, 44 and 90). Unlike other causes of coughing, there is usually no nasal discharge. A harsh, dry cough is heard both in the stable and at the beginning of exercise. Coughing usually lessens during a ride. Badly affected animals, particularly in-foal mares, can become extremely distressed with very laboured breathing. There is no effective treatment but symptoms can be prevented by attempting to produce as spore-free a stable atmosphere as possible. Drugs, similar to those used to treat asthma in humans, can be given to horses via a nebuliser and face mask. Treatment once a day for four consecutive days should prevent symptoms developing for a further three weeks.

Coughing. This can be associated with any of the respiratory virus infections. A moist cough is seen especially in infections with Equine Influenza virus and may persist for several months after the initial infection. A harsh, dry cough may be caused by Lungworm (see also page 115), but more often is due to allergy to spores in fodder and bedding (COPD, see previous paragraph). Coughing can also be a feature of Strangles. Coughing may respond to the administration of antibiotics and cough medicines when it is due to infection of the upper airways. When it is due to a lung problem (COPD or Lungworm) antibiotics will make no difference.

Enlarged Glands under the Jaw. A degree of enlargement is seen with most infection of the upper respiratory tract. In Strangles, the glands become exceptionally enlarged and may rupture to discharge pus (which is highly infectious).

Equine Influenza. This virus causes very severe 'flu-like symptoms. It can cause coughing for many weeks or months and other unwanted after-effects. Horse 'flu usually occurs in epidemics and is spread at equine events by coughing horses. The introduction of compulsory vaccination for horses taking part in many forms of equine competition has greatly reduced the risk of 'flu epidemics. Affected horses are usually very sick, with a fever, nasal discharge and cough. (See also page 134.)

Nasal Discharges. A watery nasal discharge commonly occurs with infection caused by any of several viruses that can produce 'flu-like symptoms in horses. Thicker discharges occur when secondary bacterial infection follows the initial virus disease. A thick nasal discharge from one nostril is usually a sign of sinus infection. A thick discharge from both nostrils can be a sign of Strangles.

Pleurisy. Inflammation of the lining of the chest. See "Pneumonia".

Pneumonia. Inflammation of the lungs may follow a cold or "chill". There is loss of appetite and rapid loss of flesh; fever, with inflammation of the lining of the eyes, a fast pulse and quickened breathing; constipation, and often a reddish discharge from the nose, and a cough. Usually the animal stands with his forelegs apart, and if the ribs are tapped over the lungs a dull sound is heard.

Prompt administration of antibiotics, by the vet, is essential, backed by good nursing with attention to general comfort and efforts to tempt the appetite (green food is valuable). A long rest should follow recovery.

Roaring or Whistling. This condition results from paralysis of some of the larynx muscles, which causes a characteristic inspiratory noise during fast exercise. This is known as "Roaring" or "Whistling", depending on whether it is a high or low pitched sound. What causes the nerve damage (that leads to the paralysis) is unclear, but large, long-necked horses are often affected and there is thought to be a hereditary predisposition. The obstruction of the airway can cause loss of performance, and although nothing can be done to remedy the paralysis, various operations, including the "Hobday" operation and tubing (fixing a metal tube into the windpipe through which the horse breathes), can be performed to try and improve the air-flow to the lungs.

Sinus Problems. Sinus infections are quite common in horses. A thick discharge is seen in one or, less often, both nostrils. A course of antibiotics will usually clear this up. In some cases it may be necessary to perform an operation to drain an infected sinus. Feeding a horse from a bowl at ground level encourages sinus and other nasal discharges to drain away.

Strangles. This is a highly infectious bacterial disease which is becoming increasingly common. It is characterised by fever, a thick nasal discharge, with or without a cough, but accompanied by gross enlargement of the lymph glands beneath the jaw. These usually rupture to release a highly infectious pus. Occasionally, abscesses occur in other lymph glands inside the body (called "Bastard Strangles"). This can have serious, and sometimes fatal, consequences.

Whenever Strangles is suspected the horse should be isolated immediately. It is a very infectious disease and it is preferable to isolate a horse needlessly rather than spread Strangles. Nursing and antibiotic treatment are needed and care must be taken to burn any bedding or other material contaminated by discharges. Immunity is 100% following recovery.

Virus Infections of the Upper Airways. The most common is Equine Herpes Virus Type 1 which frequently causes colds and "snotty" noses in foals and yearlings. It also causes mild 'flu-like symptoms in adult horses. These usually recover with rest but, like the human cold, immunity is short-lived and re-infection is common. This is "The Virus" which can affect the performance of racehorses and other competing horses.

INHALATIONS

In many of the foregoing complaints, steaming the nostrils is recommended. These inhalations are prepared by pouring boiling water over a handful of chaff, bran or hay in a nosebag; the vapour can be medicated by adding a teaspoonful of Friar's Balsam, spirits of camphor, terebene, etc. The nosebag should be worn for 10–15 minutes, three times daily. A bucket may be used, with a blanket or sack loosely surrounding the nose to gain full benefit from the vapour but to admit some air as well.

AILMENTS WITH DIGESTIVE SYMPTOMS

Choke. In this condition the horse is found arching its neck and making repeated attempts to swallow. It may also cough and drool saliva and food may appear at the nostrils. A common cause is sugar beet cubes that have been insufficiently soaked (see page 94). Large unchewed pieces of vegetable, such as apples or carrots, or concentrate cubes that have been swallowed without being chewed, may all become lodged in the gullet. The vet should be called immediately, but the horse can be offered water while waiting for him to arrive. A muscle relaxant, given by injection, will usually allow the food to pass on down but may take some time to work. Large flat stones can be placed in the manger of greedy feeders to slow their eating and prevent Choke.

Colic. This is a term for any pain arising within the abdomen. In horses this usually refers to pain arising in the bowels, although kidney pain (Renal Colic) is also possible. A horse's abdominal contents are very well supplied with nerve endings – so much so that it is highly susceptible to pain and makes as much fuss about the mildest indigestion as it would for a major abdominal catastrophe, such as a ruptured bowel. For this reason, it is very difficult for the person looking after the horse to know when something serious is wrong. Thus all cases of Colic should be treated as emergencies and the vet should be called immediately. In most instances, all that is required is a pain-killing injection. In the case where there is something seriously wrong – such as a Twisted Gut – if this can be detected early and prompt action taken, the horse's life may be saved.

In colic, the pain is often intense. The animal is usually sweating, constantly pawing, and turning its head towards its belly or striking at it with a hindfoot. There may be drum-like distension (Flatulent Colic), and the animal shows signs of distress and uneasiness. In severe cases he often lies down and rises repeatedly, and may roll continually – when there is danger of twisting or knotting of the intestines. If it is attempting to roll, a bridle should be put on the horse and it can be walked quietly. This may ease the pain until the vet arrives. However, this should not be overdone so as to exhaust the horse. During this time someone else should make up a deep straw bed in the largest box available. There are various types of Colic which may require different forms of treatment.

Colic, Flatulent. The pain arises from excessive fermentation and accumulation of gas in the bowels. This often occurs as a result of over-eating or sudden changes in diet. Tinkling and gurgling sounds can usually be heard and the horse may pass wind. Pain-killers are normally given to reduce pain and stop the animal from rolling; this can be dangerous with a tight, gas-filled bowel which could possibly rupture. In addition, the vet will usually administer, by stomach tube, drugs to prevent fermentation, together with laxatives.

Colic, Spasmodic. In this, the pain comes in spasms. These last for three or four hours, after which the horse appears better, only to have the pain return a few hours later. In most cases this condition results from interference with the blood supply to the bowels caused by current or previous damage by worms. (Aneurysms are more serious and are caused when large blood vessels become completely blocked. See page 140.) Worms have been found to be responsible for up to 90% of all colic cases. Treatment involves giving pain-killers and intensive worm treatment.

Enteritis (Diarrhoea). Diarrhoea caused by bacterial infection is quite common in foals. Any foal with a scour should receive immediately veterinary attention. Septicaemia may follow Diarrhoea in foals, and antibiotics should always be given. Loose dropping and diarrhoea in adult horses are very uncommon unless associated with worms, and can be serious, as extensive fluid loss will cause shock. A vet should be called immediately to treat any mature horse suffering in this way. It may be necessary to give large volumes of intravenous fluid to overcome shock and save the animal's life.

In rare cases, persistent sloppy droppings may be due to chronic bowel damage, resulting in thickening of the large intestine wall, which is then less able to reabsorb water from the gut contents. Such animals are also less able to absorb nutrients and tend to be "poor doers". The bowel damage can be detected on a simple blood test which is usually carried out when horses are losing condition with no satisfactory explanation.

Grass Sickness. This disease is only found in certain localities. In this condition there is a gradual progressive paralysis of the bowel, which eventually stops working altogether. The large intestines become impacted with food, while saliva and gastric secretions accumulate in the stomach. Eventually, stomach contents are regurgitated down the nostrils (hence the name "Grass Sickness") or the stomach ruptures, with fatal consequences. Initially, this disease resembles other types of Colic. It is invariably fatal and in spite of intensive research its cause remains unknown.

Gross Over-eating. Horses breaking into the feed store and gorging concentrates can become seriously ill. Flatulent Colic, purging accompanied by shock, and acute Laminitis can all follow. This must be prevented by keeping the food store shut and locked at all times. A plastic dustbin, with a lid that can be held in place by clips, is an ideal store for opened bags of nuts or cubes and is an extra safety precaution. If this eventually does occur, it is best to call the vet immediately. Drugs given by stomach tube may help prevent serious problems developing.

Impaction (Constipation). This is a common problem in stabled horses. It is often caused by a combination of too much dry food, too little water intake and insufficient exercise. The pain is usually dull; droppings will be hard or absent, and the animal may refuse food. Laxatives are normally given by the vet, by stomach tube, and these may sometimes take several days to work through the system to relieve the "stoppage". Because of their mild laxative effect, bran mashes and green foods are

Connemara

normally included in the diet of stabled horses to prevent this problem. Salt licks or the addition of salt to the diet may also stimulate sufficient water intake. If droppings are hard, 30–120 gms (1–4 oz) of Epsom Salts (Magnesium Sulphate) – depending on the horse's size – added to the food or drinking water should prevent Impaction and Colic.

"Twisted Gut". This happens when one portion of bowel becomes twisted around, and trapped, by another. It may be the initial cause of Colic, but more often than not it is brought about by the horse rolling in an effort to relieve the pain of some other form of Colic. The pain of a "Twisted Gut" is usually very acute and is not relieved by pain-killers. Signs of shock are soon evident (a rapid, thready pulse and blue-tinged membranes). If a twist can be detected early and corrected by surgery, the horse may recover. If there is too long a delay, the horse will die of shock. The possibility of a twist is the reason why vets like to monitor all Colic cases carefully.

USEFUL ADDRESSES

British Horse Society (B.H.S.), British Equestrian Centre, Stoneleigh, Kenilworth, Warwicks, CV8 2LR (Tel: 0203–696697).

Addresses of individual horse and pony associations and breed societies can be obtained from the B.H.S. who also produce a wide range of equestrian publications.

Royal College of Veterinary Surgeons, 32 Belgrave Square, London, SW1X 9QP (Tel: 01–235 4971).

A booklet entitled "Colours and Markings of Horses" is available, at a nominal cost, from the Royal College of Veterinary Surgeons. It gives detailed descriptions of the colours and markings of British horses for identification purposes. Specific identification of individual animals is essential for those needing vaccination certificates (see page 134) when entering certain events and competitions.

Association of British Riding Schools, Old Brewery Yard, Penzance, Cornwall, TR18 2SL.

British Bloodstock Agency, 14 Pall Mall, London, SW1Y 5LU.

British Field Sports Society, 59 Kennington Road, London, SE1 7PZ.

Federation Equestre Internationale (F.E.I.), British Equestrian Centre, Stoneleigh, Kenilworth, Warwicks, CV8 2LR.

International League for the Protection of Horses, 67a Camden High Street, London, N.W.1.

The Jockey Club, 42 Portman Square, London, W1H 0EN.

National Association of Farriers and Blacksmiths, Avenue R, 7th Street, National Agricultural Centre, Stoneleigh, Kenilworth, Warwicks, CV8 2LG.

Royal Veterinary College, Royal College Street, London, NW1 0TU.

The Worshipful Company of Saddlers, Saddlers Hall, Gutter Lane, Cheapside, London, EC2V 6BR.

PERIODICALS OF INTEREST

"Horse & Hound". IPC Magazines Ltd., King's Reach Tower, Stamford Street, London, SE1 9LS.

"Pony", *"Horse & Rider"*. D. J. Murphy (Publishers) Ltd., 296 Ewell Road, Surbiton, Surrey, KT6 7AQ.

"Pony Club", *"Carriage Driving"*, *"Dressage Review"*. EPB Publications Ltd, Warwick House, Banbury Road, Southam, Warwicks, CV33 0HJ.

"The Rider". The Riding Clubs Office, British Horse Society, British Equestrian Centre, Stoneleigh, Kenilworth, Warwicks, CV8 2LR.

"Riding". Scott Publications Ltd., Corner House, Foston, Grantham, Lincs, NG32 2JU.

"Your Horse", *"Horse & Pony"*. EMAP Pursuit Publishing, Bretton Court, Bretton, Peterborough, PE3 8DZ.

INDEX

OTHER PAPERFRONTS FOR HORSE LOVERS

All uniform with this book

THE RIGHT WAY TO RIDE A HORSE

Also by W. H. Walter, it gives simple instructions and explanations on riding. He writes just as he would talk if he was giving private tuition.

SOLVE YOUR HORSE AND PONY PROBLEMS

Authors Karen Bush and Sarah Viccars concentrate on the *everyday* problems of horse keeping. Illustrated questions and answers provide quick access to solutions.

BUYING AND FITTING SADDLERY

Also by Karen Bush and Sarah Viccars, it gives simple answers to all your equipment questions.

THE RIGHT WAY TO KEEP PONIES

Veterinary surgeon Hugh Venables gives excellent guidance on all aspects of keeping ponies.

ELLIOT RIGHT WAY BOOKS, KINGSWOOD, SURREY, U.K.